Dwayne's Guitar Lessons Presents:

Beginner's Guide to Electric Guitar Mastery

A Journey from Novice to Professional

By
Guitar Teacher
Dwayne Jenkins

Published by Tritone Publishing.

Introduction

The electric guitar is more than just a musical instrument; it's a cultural icon that has shaped the soundscape of modern music. From rock and blues to jazz, metal, and beyond, the electric guitar offers a versatile and dynamic range of sounds.

Its ability to produce everything from gentle melodies to powerful, driving riffs makes it an essential instrument for those looking to explore the vast world of contemporary electric music.

Learning to play the electric guitar can be an incredibly rewarding experience. For many, it offers a creative outlet and a means of self-expression. Whether you're strumming simple chords or crafting intricate solos, the guitar provides a platform for expressing your emotions and ideas.

The sense of accomplishment that comes from mastering a new riff or song can boost your confidence and improve your overall well-being. Moreover, the electric guitar is an accessible instrument for beginners because the basics can be learned and performed fairly easily.

The "Beginner's Guide to Electric Guitar Mastery" is your comprehensive roadmap to becoming a proficient electric guitarist. Whether you're a beginner or have played it before, this guide is designed to take you on an exciting journey.

This guide is structured to provide a step-by-step approach to mastering the electric guitar. It covers fundamental topics, including choosing the right guitar and accessories, essential playing techniques, and music theory.

As you progress, you'll delve into more advanced topics, including improvisation, effects, and playing in a band. Each chapter builds on the previous ones, ensuring a comprehensive learning experience.

As you immerse yourself in the lessons and techniques presented in this guide, you'll not only develop technical proficiency but also deepen your appreciation for music. Embrace the challenges and triumphs that come with learning an instrument, and enjoy the personal growth that accompanies your musical journey. Have fun and enjoy the process.

Sincerely, Dwayne Jenkins

Table of Contents

Chapter I: Getting Started With the Electric

Lesson 1: Choosing Your First Electric Guitar

Selecting your first electric guitar is an exciting step in your musical journey. The right guitar can inspire you to practice and improve, while the wrong one might make learning more difficult than it needs to be.

That is why we will begin here. This lesson will guide you through the process of choosing a guitar that suits your style, budget, and preferences.

Types of Electric Guitars

Electric guitars come in various shapes, sizes, and styles, each offering a unique sound and feel. Here are some of the most common types:

1. **Solid-Body Guitars:** The most popular type of electric guitar, known for their versatility and durability. They are often used in rock, pop, and metal genres. Examples include the Fender Stratocaster and Gibson Les Paul.

1. **Hollow-Body Guitars**: These guitars feature a fully hollow body, which produces a warm, resonant sound. They are often used in jazz and blues music. The Gibson ES-335 is a well-known example.
2. **Semi-Hollow Body Guitars**: Combining elements of both solid and hollow bodies, these guitars have a center block to reduce feedback while retaining some of the warmth and resonance of a hollow body. The Epiphone Dot is a popular choice among semi-hollow body guitars.

Choosing the right guitar involves more than just picking a type. Consider the following factors to ensure you make a wise investment:

- **Budget**: Determine how much you're willing to spend. While it's tempting to go for the cheapest option, investing in a quality guitar can provide better playability and sound, encouraging you to practice more.

- **Comfort and Playability**: Try out different guitars to find one that feels comfortable to hold and play. Consider the weight, neck shape, and fretboard width.
- **Sound Quality**: Listen to the tone of different guitars. Even among similar types, each guitar has a unique sound. Choose one that matches your musical style.
- **Brand and Reputation**: Some brands are known for their quality and reliability. Conduct research and seek recommendations to identify reputable brands that produce well-crafted instruments.
- **Aesthetic Appeal**: While not the most important factor, choosing a guitar that appeals to you visually can boost your motivation. Look for a finish and design that inspires you.

By understanding the types of electric guitars and considering these key factors, you can make an informed decision and select a guitar that will be a loyal companion on your musical journey.

Lesson 2: Essential Guitar Accessories

Equipping yourself with the right accessories can enhance your playing experience and ensure you make the most of your practice sessions. This lesson will cover the essential accessories every beginner electric guitarist should consider.

Picks, Straps, and Cables

- **Picks**: Guitar picks, or plectrums, come in various shapes, sizes, and materials. Experiment with different thicknesses and materials to find the one that suits your playing style and comfort level. Picks can impact your tone and the ease with which you play.

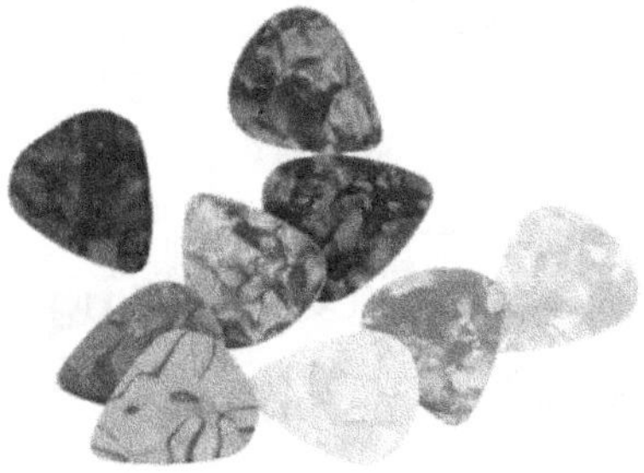

Straps: A comfortable guitar strap is crucial, especially if you plan to play standing up. Look for adjustable straps made from durable materials. Consider padded straps for extra comfort during long practice sessions or performances.

- **Cables:** Quality guitar cables are essential for maintaining a clear, uninterrupted signal from your guitar to your amplifier. Look for cables with sturdy connectors and shielding to minimize interference.

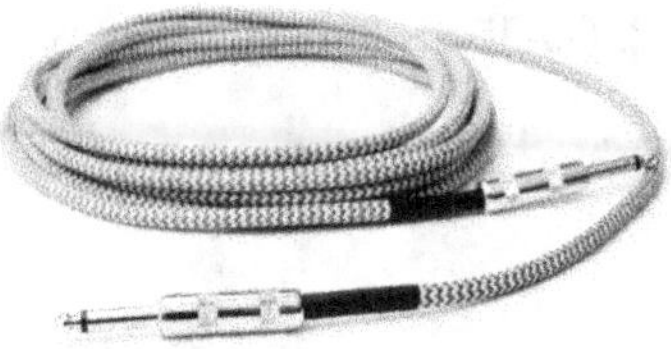

Amplifiers and Effects Pedals

- **Amplifiers**: Essential for electric guitar players, they enhance and project your instrument's sound. When choosing an amplifier, consider the size, wattage, and features that fit your practice space and musical goals.
- **Effects Pedals**: Add variety and depth to your sound. While it's easy to get overwhelmed by options, start with a few basic pedals such as distortion, overdrive, or reverb. These can enhance your sound and enable creative exploration.

Investing in the right accessories can significantly impact your playing experience and enjoyment. As you progress, you'll discover which tools best complement your style and enhance your musical expression.

Lesson 3: Setting Up Your Guitar

Properly setting up your guitar is essential for ensuring it plays well and sounds its best. It involves a few key tasks that can significantly improve your playing experience. Let's dive into the basics of tuning and maintaining your electric guitar.

Tuning Your Guitar

Tuning is the first step in setting up your guitar and should be done every time before you play. An out-of-tune guitar can hinder your ability to learn and play effectively.

- **Standard Tuning**: The most common tuning for electric guitars is E-A-D-G-B-E, from the thickest (6th) to the thinnest (1st) string. Electronic tuners or tuner apps are best used to provide precise feedback.

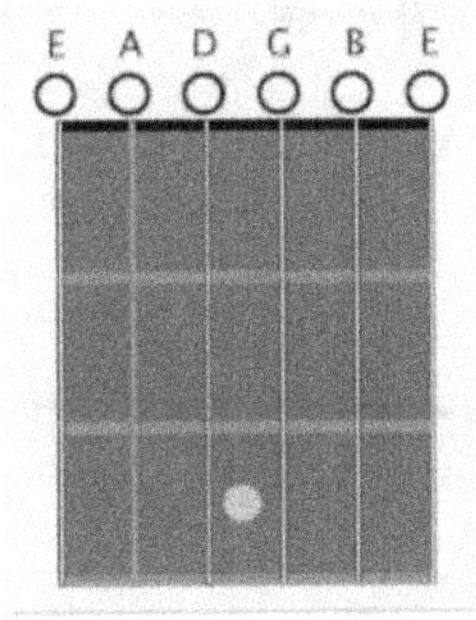

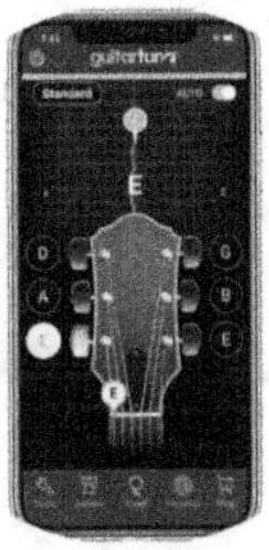

- **Tuning Stability**: Ensure your guitar stays in tune by stretching new strings after installation and regularly checking the tension on the tuning pegs. Properly wound strings around the tuning posts can also enhance tuning stability.

As you progress, explore tunings such as Drop D, Open G, or DADGAD. These tunings can give your playing a unique sound and feel and are often used in specific genres or songs.

Basic Guitar Maintenance

Maintaining your guitar is crucial for its longevity and optimal performance. Here are some basic maintenance tips you should follow:

- **String Changes**: Regularly changing your strings can improve your guitar's sound and playability. Old strings can become dull and challenging to play. Change strings every few months when you notice a decline in sound quality.

- **Cleaning Your Guitar**: Use a soft cloth to wipe down your guitar after playing to remove sweat and oils that can damage the finish. Occasionally, use a guitar-specific cleaner and polish to maintain the wood's condition.

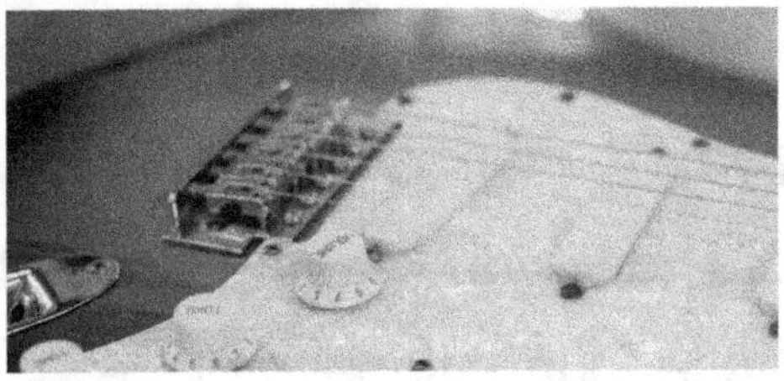

- **Neck and Action Adjustments**: The neck's curvature, also known as the relief, is designed to provide clearance for string vibration. If this is out of sync, it can affect playability.

If you notice fret buzz or have difficulty playing the strings, consider adjusting the truss rod or bridge. It's often best to consult a professional to handle these adjustments,

Pickup Maintenance: Keep pickups free of dust and debris. If you're experiencing sound issues, checking the pickup height or connections may be necessary.

You can easily make these adjustments to suit your playing style.

By regularly tuning and maintaining your guitar, you'll ensure it remains in excellent condition and provides you with the best possible playing experience. With these foundations in place, you're ready to dive deeper into your musical journey.

Chapter I Quiz

In Chapter 1, we covered the basics. These are what will develop your foundation. Get this right, and all else will fall into place.

Q: What are the three main types of electric guitars?
A: ______________________________

Q: Why are budget, comfort, and sound quality important?
A: ______________________________

Q: How is experimenting with different guitars beneficial?
A: ______________________________

Q: How do amplifiers and effects pedals enhance your tone?
A: ______________________________

Q: Why is it crucial to make sure your guitar is in tune?
A: ______________________________

Q: Why is guitar maintenance important for your performance?
A: ______________________________

Chapter I Summary

First, make sure you find the right guitar and amplifier. This will inspire and motivate you to practice and improve. At the same time, the wrong ones can make learning difficult and frustrate you. So, make sure to take the time to get this right.

Second, research guitar and amp types, and try a few at your local music store. Each will be slightly different and offer alternative options, which can make a significant difference in your progress.

Third, ensure you have the right accessories, such as guitar picks, a tuner, cables, and a guitar strap. The right pick will make all the difference, so make sure to try a few out for the best results.

Fourth, setting up your guitar for maximum performance. This means learning how to tune it with your tuner. The most important lesson to master.

Lastly, ensure you understand basic guitar maintenance. The better you know your guitar, the better you will be able to play it. Being a great guitar player means making an intimate connection with the instrument.

Chapter II: Understanding Music Theory

Lesson 4: The Basics of Music Theory

Understanding music theory is essential for any musician, as it provides the foundation for creating and interpreting music. In this lesson, we'll cover the fundamental concepts that will allow you to understand how music is structured.

Notes and Scales

Notes are the building blocks of music. On the guitar, each fret corresponds to a different note. Understanding how these notes work together is crucial for playing melodies and harmonies.

- **The Musical Alphabet**: Music uses the first seven letters of the alphabet: A, B, C, D, E, F, and G. These letters represent the white keys on a piano, and they repeat in cycles called octaves.

In addition to these seven letters, you have accidentals. These are notes between these seven letters. This is also called the chromatic scale, which makes up twelve notes altogether.

- **Sharps and Flats**: Between most of the natural notes, there are additional notes called sharps (#) and flats (b). A sharp raises a note by a half step, while a flat lowers it.

For example, the note between A and B can be called A# (A sharp) or Bb (B flat).

- **Major and Minor Scales**: These are the most common types of scales in Western music. The major scale has a bright and happy sound, while the minor scale typically sounds more somber.

The minor sounds different because the notes in the scale formula are altered. The major scale has all natural notes, whereas the minor scale has a flat 3rd, flat 6th, and a flat 7th. This is what gives it its tone structure.

Learning the patterns for these scales on the guitar will aid in both improvisation and songwriting. This will be discussed further in this training.

Understanding Chords

Chords are groups of notes played together, and they form the harmonic foundation of most music. .Understanding how chords are constructed will help you in creating chord progressions and accompanying melodies.

- **Triads**: The simplest chords are triads, which consist of three notes: the root, third, and fifth. These notes are derived from scales. For instance, a C major triad consists of the notes C, E, and G.

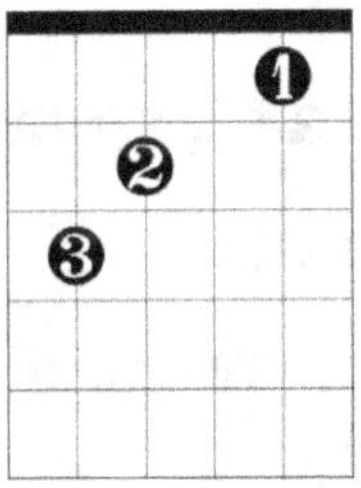
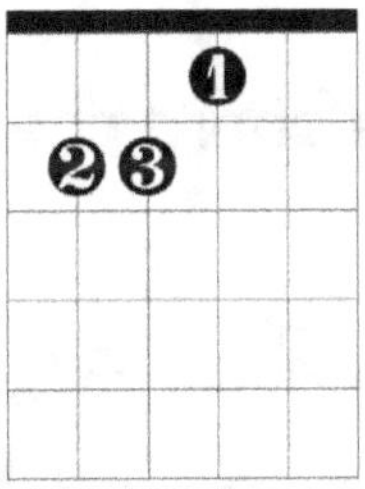
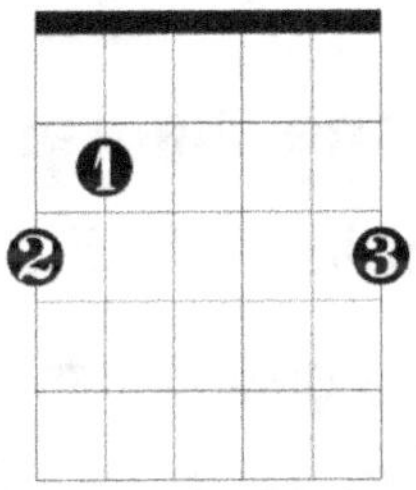

- **Chord Quality**: Chords can be major, minor, diminished, or augmented, depending on the intervals between their notes. Each quality has a distinct sound and emotional effect.

*You want to master the emotion that each chord produces.

Lesson 5: Reading Chord Charts and Guitar Tabs

Understanding how to read chord charts and guitar tabs is a crucial skill for any guitarist. These tools provide a visual representation of music, allowing you to learn songs efficiently and accurately.

Reading Chord Charts

Chord charts are a simplified way to represent chords, showing you where to place your fingers on the fretboard. Here's how to read them effectively:

- **Understanding the Diagram:** A chord chart is a grid that represents the guitar's fretboard. The vertical lines correspond to the strings, from the low E (left) to the high E (right). The horizontal lines represent the frets.

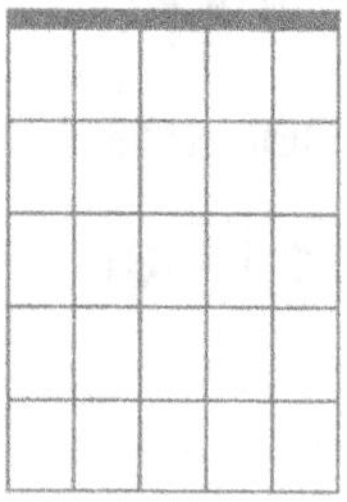

Chord chart example.

- **Finger Placement:** Dots on the grid indicate where to place your fingers. Numbers inside the dots correspond to the fingers you should use: 1 for the index, 2 for the middle, 3 for the ring, and 4 for the pinky.

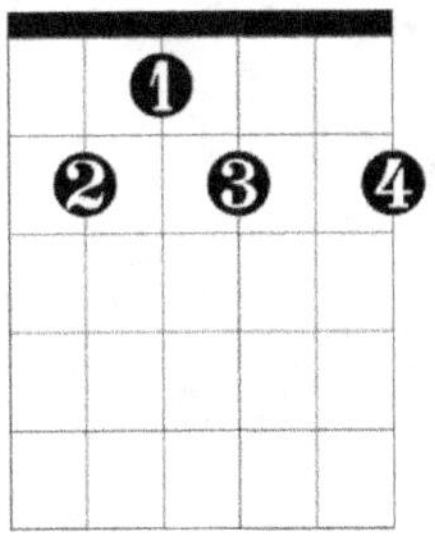

The B7 chord chart.

- **Chord Variations:** Chord charts often show different variations of the same chord, allowing you to choose the version that best suits your playing style or the song's requirements.

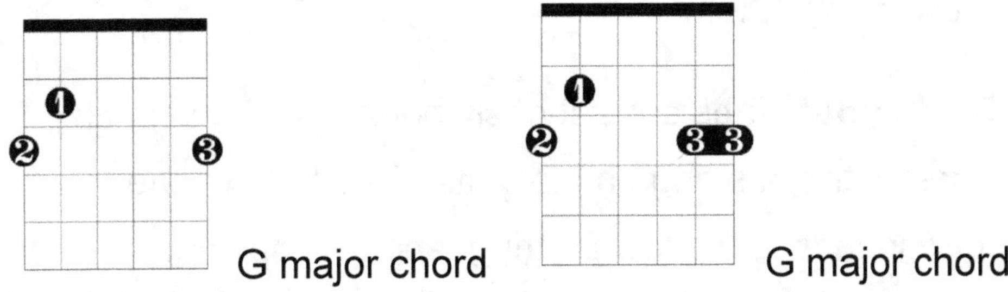

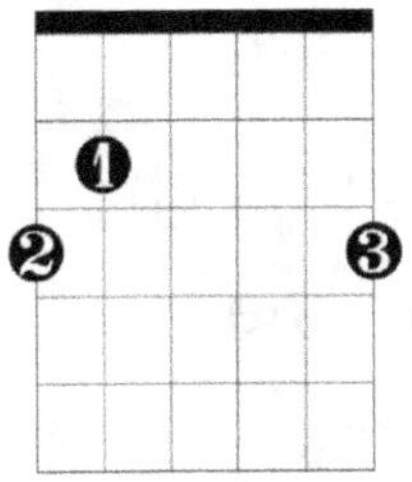

G major chord

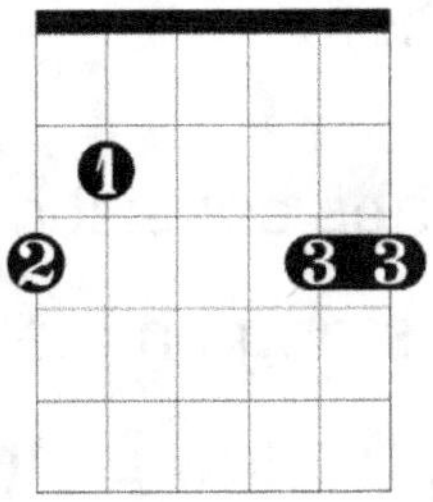

G major chord

Notice how these two chords are similar, but slightly different.

- **Practice Tip:** Start by familiarizing yourself with basic open chords such as C, G, D, and E minor. Practice moving between these chords to develop smooth transitions.

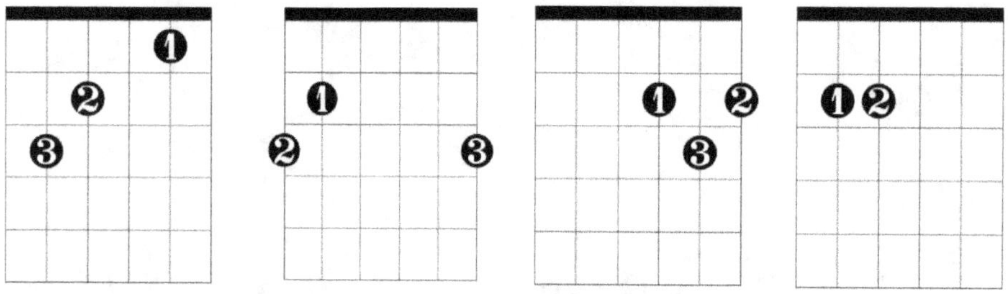

Understanding Guitar Tabs

Guitar tabs, or tablature, provide a detailed representation of how to play melodies, solos, and riffs. Unlike traditional sheet music, tabs are specifically designed for stringed instruments. Here's how to read them:

- **The Layout:** Tabs consist of six horizontal lines, each representing a string on the guitar. The bottom line corresponds to the low E string, and the top line represents the high E string.

- **The Layout:** Tabs consist of six horizontal lines, each representing a guitar string. The bottom line corresponds to the low E string, and the top line represents the high E string.

- **Fret Numbers:** Numbers on the lines indicate which fret to press on the corresponding string. For example, a "5" on the fifth line means you should play the fifth fret of the A string.

- **Reading Rhythm:** While tabs show what to play, they don't indicate rhythm. Listen to the song or refer to the sheet music to understand the timing and rhythm of the notes.

Tabs are like a shortcut to reading traditional music. They give you the basics, but not everything.

- **Techniques and Symbols:** Tabs may include symbols for specific techniques, such as hammer-ons, pull-offs, and slides. Below are some examples of these techniques.

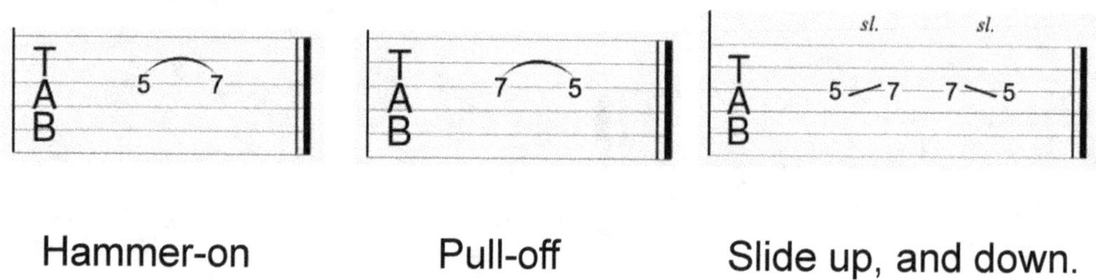

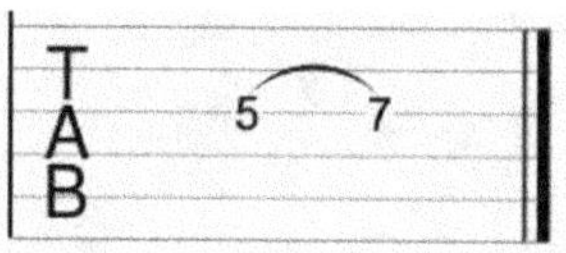

Hammer-on

Pull-off

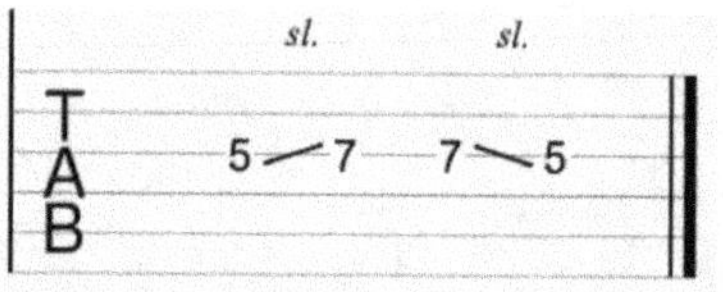

Slide up, and down.

Just like standard notation, you'll need to familiarize yourself with these symbols to accurately interpret the tab.

- **Practice Tip:** Begin with simple tabs for well-known songs. Focus on playing accurately and at a slow tempo before gradually increasing your speed.

By mastering chord charts and guitar tabs, you'll gain the ability to learn songs quickly and expand your repertoire. These tools are invaluable for any guitarist, providing a visual guide to playing music and enhancing your overall musicianship.

With patience and practice, you'll develop the confidence and skill to tackle more complex pieces and express yourself creatively on the guitar.

Lesson 6: Establishing Rhythm and Timing

Mastering rhythm and timing is crucial for any guitarist, as they form the backbone of music and ensure your playing is coherent and engaging. In this lesson, we'll explore the fundamentals of these concepts, helping you build a solid foundation that enhances your overall musicality.

Time Signatures

Understanding time signatures is key to playing music rhythmically and with the correct feel. Here's what you need to know:

- **What Are Time Signatures?**
  A time signature indicates how many beats are in each measure and what note value constitutes one beat. It appears at the beginning of a piece of music.

This indicates rhythm and timing in a piece of music when using standard notation.

- **Common Time Signatures**
  - **4/4 Time**: Known as "common time," this is the most frequently used time signature. It means there are four beats per measure, and a quarter note gets one beat.
  - **3/4 Time**: Often used in waltzes, this signature has three beats per measure, with the quarter note again getting one beat.
  - **6/8 Time**: This gives a more flowing, compound meter feel, with six beats per measure and the eighth note receiving one beat.

- **Counting Beats**

  Practice counting the beats aloud while playing to internalize the rhythm. Start with clapping or tapping your foot to the beat, then incorporate your guitar playing.

Remember, different time signatures allow you to create with various rhythms and timing. The most common is 4/4, so start there before proceeding to other time signatures.

Mastering Strum Patterns

Strumming patterns are essential for creating rhythm and texture in your playing. Let's explore some basic techniques:

- **Basic Strum Patterns:** Begin with simple patterns in 4/4 time, such as:
- **Down, Down, Down, Down**: This pattern is versatile and works well in many songs.
- **Down-Up, Down-Up, Down-Up, Down-Up**: A consistent, flowing pattern that is great for faster tempos.

Strum down on each beat: 1 2 3 4.

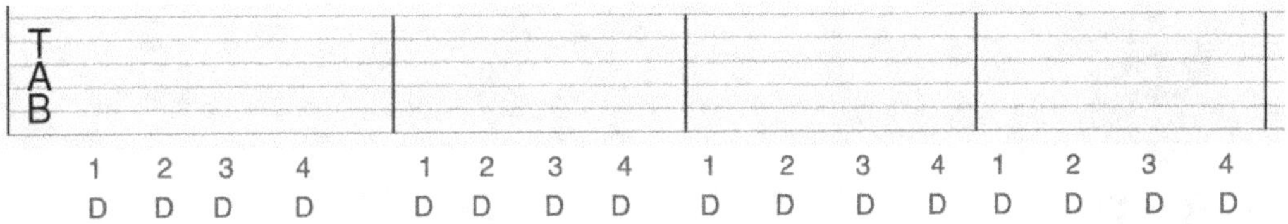

Strum down on 1 and 3 and up on 2 and 4.

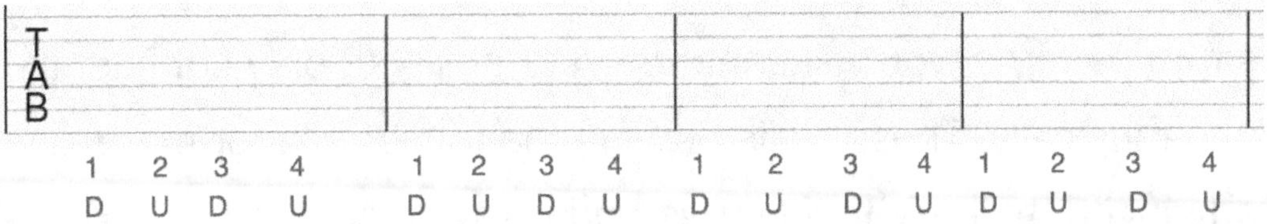

Notice how these two patterns create different rhythms.

- **Syncopation and Accents:** Experiment with emphasizing different beats or parts of a pattern to create syncopation, which can add interest and groove to your playing.

Many great songs that catch your attention when you listen to them incorporate this technique, drawing you in.

- **Practicing with a Metronome:** Use a metronome to maintain precise timing. Start slow and gradually increase the tempo as you become more comfortable with each pattern.

By developing a strong sense of rhythm and mastering various strum patterns, you will enhance your ability to play confidently and musically. These skills provide the foundation for more advanced rhythmic techniques and will greatly contribute to your overall guitar proficiency.

Chapter II Quiz

In Chapter 2, you have learned about music theory basics, chord charts and guitar tabs, and rhythm and timing. All are critical to foundational development.

Q: What are the seven letters of the musical alphabet?
A: ____

Q: What is another name for the musical alphabet?
A: ____

Q: What is the benefit of learning to read chord charts?
A: ____

Q: How do guitar tabs differ from chord charts?
A: ____

Q: Why are strumming patterns beneficial to guitar playing?
A: ____

Q: Why is it beneficial to play with a metronome?
A: ____

Chapter II Summary

First, understand the importance of music theory. This is essential for any guitarist, as it provides the foundation for interpreting and creating music. Learning and applying this knowledge will enhance your guitar playing.

Second, make sure you fully understand the notes of the musical alphabet, sharps and flats, chords, and major and minor scales. These will provide the foundation for understanding songs and crafting your own compositions.

Third, learn to read chord charts and guitar tabs. These tools provide a visual representation of music, allowing you to gain insight into songs and their components. This will enable you to explore more complex musical landscapes.

Fourth, develop rhythm and timing. This is crucial for any guitarist. This forms the backbone of most songs and provides a solid foundation and understanding of the basics of music.

Lastly, by developing a strong sense of rhythm and timing, you will be able to play and craft music with greater confidence. Allowing you to improve your musicianship and set a solid foundation for future lessons to come.

Chapter III: Basic Guitar Techniques

Lesson 7: Finger Placement and Hand Positions

Mastering finger placement and hand positions is fundamental for any guitarist. Whether you're playing chords, scales, or intricate solos, proper technique ensures you play comfortably and minimizes the risk of injury.

Fretting Hand Techniques

Your fretting hand plays a crucial role in producing clear, articulate notes. Here are some essential tips to optimize your fretting hand technique:

- **Proper Finger Placement**: Position your fingers close to the fret, but not directly on it, to minimize buzzing and achieve a clean sound. Ensure your fingers are pressing down firmly enough to produce a clear note.

- **Finger Independence:** Practice exercises that promote finger independence to enhance your dexterity. This includes playing scales or finger exercises slowly and deliberately, focusing on moving each finger individually.

With this exercise below, use all four fingers to play each note individually. Start at the 5th fret on the low E string and proceed through the pattern on all six strings.

- **Hand Position**: Keep your thumb behind the neck, roughly opposite your middle finger. This provides stability and allows your fingers to stretch across the fretboard. Avoid gripping the neck too tightly, as this can limit your range of motion.

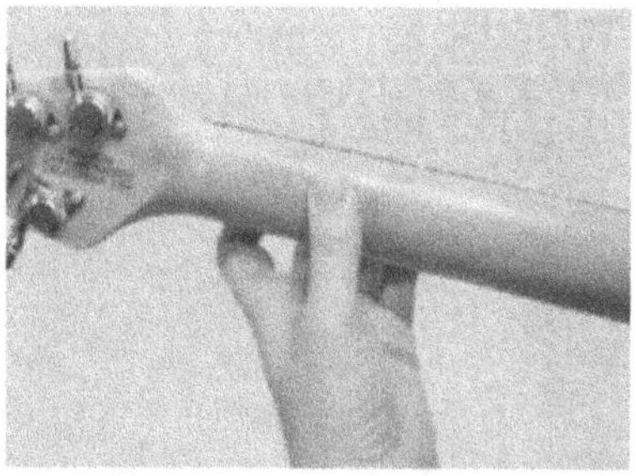

- **Avoiding Strain:** Maintain a relaxed hand posture to prevent tension. Take breaks during practice to stretch your fingers and hands, reducing the risk of strain or injury.

Picking Hand Techniques

Your picking hand controls the rhythm and dynamics of your playing. Whether you use a pick or your fingers, mastering these techniques is vital for producing a consistent and expressive sound:

- **Holding the Pick**: Grip the pick between your thumb and index finger, leaving a small portion exposed. Experiment with angles and grip pressure to find what feels comfortable and provides the best control.

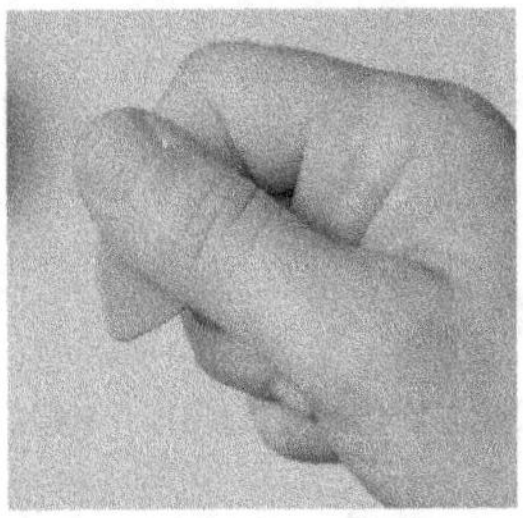

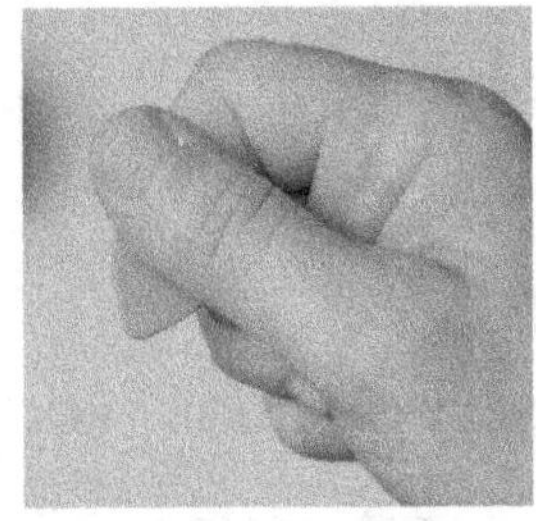

Finding the right pick for your playing style will make all the difference in your overall tone. Experiment with different ones.

- **Picking Motion:** Use a combination of wrist and forearm movements. Keep your movements small and controlled to maintain precision and speed. Practice daily to achieve fluidity and consistency.

- **Fingerpicking**: If you prefer fingerstyle, use your thumb for the bass strings (E, A, D) and your index, middle, and ring fingers for the treble strings (G, B, E). Practice fingerpicking patterns to develop coordination and independence among your fingers.

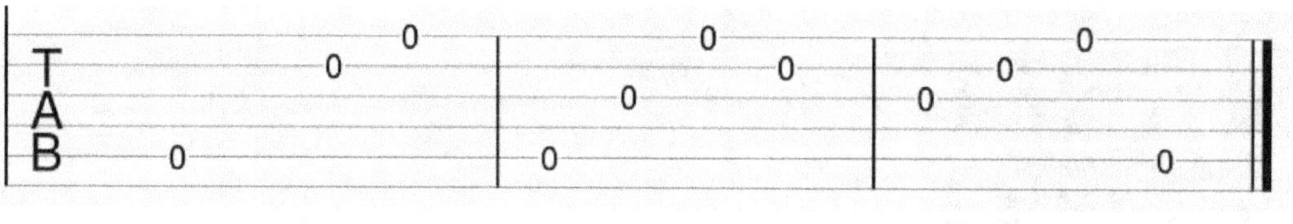

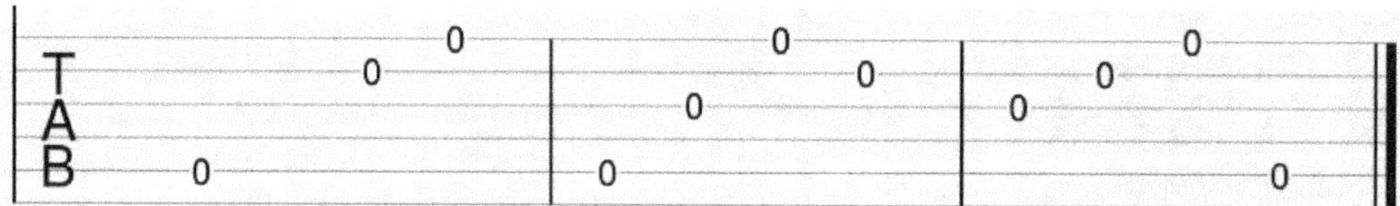

By focusing on proper finger placement and hand positions, you will build a solid technical foundation that will support your development as a master guitarist.

Lesson 8: Basic Chords and Progressions

Understanding and mastering basic chords and progressions is essential for any guitarist. These foundational elements form the backbone of countless songs across various genres. In this lesson, we will explore open chords and barre chords.

Open Chords

Open chords are among the first chords guitarists learn. They are called "open" because they involve open strings that are not fretted. The most common open chords should help you build your chord vocabulary.

C Major, A minor, G Major, E minor, and D Major.

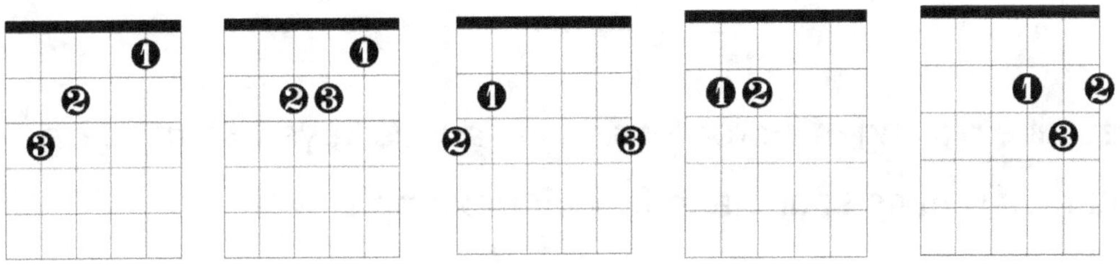

Mastering these open chords will allow you to play many simple songs and will serve as a foundation for creating chord progressions.

Chord Progressions

Chord progressions are when you chords together in a sequence. As a guitarist, fully understanding this concept will enable you to play a wide range of music and even craft your own compositions.

- **I-IV-V Progression:** This is one of the most common progressions in music. It is foundational in genres such as rock and blues. In the key of C major, this progression would consist of the chords C (I), F (IV), and G (V).

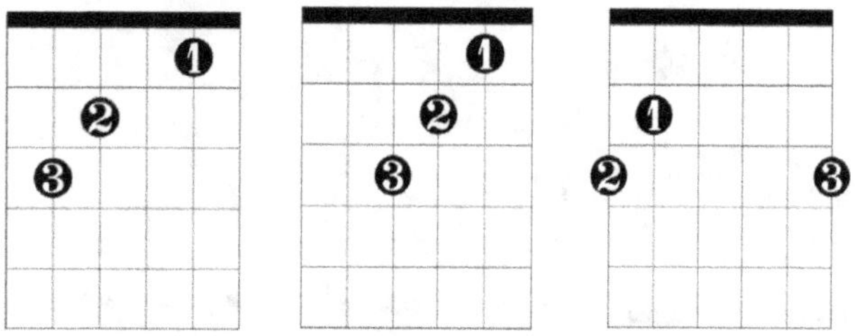

Practice playing this progression in various keys to familiarize yourself with its sound and feel. For example;

Key of G major would be: G (I), C (IV), and D (V).

Key of A major would be: A (I), D (IV), and E (V).

- **ii-V-I Progression:** This progression is a staple of jazz music and is used to create smooth, satisfying resolutions. In the key of C major, the ii-V-I progression consists of the chords Dm (ii), G (V), and C (I). Mastering this progression will enhance your understanding of jazz harmony and improve your ability to navigate complex chord changes.

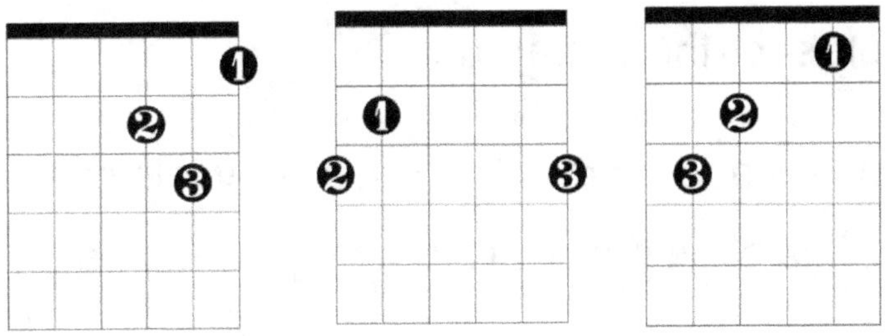

- **I-vi-IV-V Progression:** Also known as the "50s progression," this sequence was popularized in early rock and roll and doo-wop music. In the key of G major, it consists of G (I), Em (vi), C (IV), and D (V). Practice this progression to capture the nostalgic feel of classic hits.

Try these out in different keys as well, and you'll begin to hear bits and pieces of popular songs.

- **Blues Progression (12-Bar Blues):** A fundamental progression in blues music, the 12-bar blues typically follows the pattern I-I-I-I, IV-IV-I-I, V-IV-I-I. In the key of G major, this would be G (I), C (IV), and D (V). Understanding this progression will allow you to play and improvise in blues and rock settings.

Play the G chord four times, the C chord two times, the G chord two times, the D chord one time, the C chord one time, and the C, C sharp, and D chords for the turnaround.

Notice how these numbers add up to 12. That is why it is called a 12-bar progression. It is played over 12 bars or measures.

By practicing these chord progressions, you'll gain the ability to play a wide variety of songs and develop a deeper understanding of musical structure.

As you become more comfortable with these progressions, try experimenting by creating your own variations or incorporating them into your songwriting.

Lesson 9: Arpeggios and Fingerstyle

Arpeggios and fingerstyle techniques are essential for adding depth and complexity to your guitar playing. Mastering these skills allows you to create rich, textured sounds and play a wide variety of musical styles.

Understanding Arpeggios

Arpeggios are broken chords where the notes are played sequentially rather than simultaneously. They are foundational in guitar playing, providing melodic and harmonic interest. Here's how to get started with arpeggios:

- **Basic Arpeggio Shapes**: Familiarize yourself with simple major and minor arpeggio shapes. For instance, a C major arpeggio consists of the notes C, E, and G. Practice playing these notes individually across different positions on the fretboard.

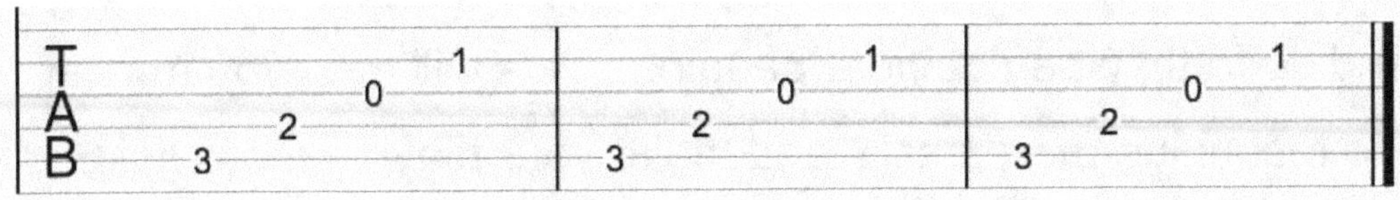

- **Finger Independence:** Use alternate picking or fingerstyle to play arpeggios, focusing on clean, even note production. Develop finger independence by practicing slowly and gradually increasing speed as you gain confidence.

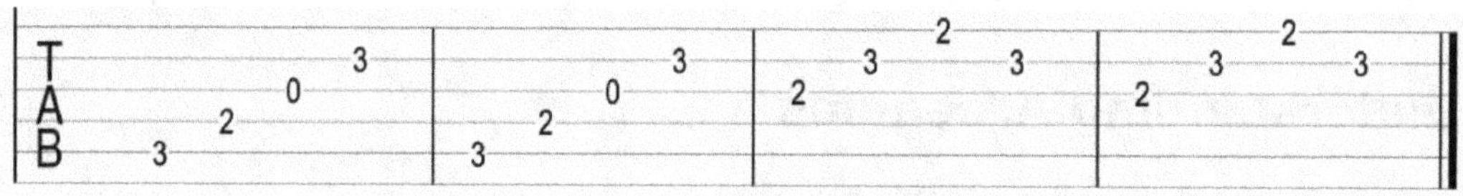

- **Chord Progressions**: Apply arpeggios to chord progressions to add variation and interest. For example, in a simple progression using the D and A major chords, outline each chord with its respective arpeggio to create a flowing, melodic accompaniment.

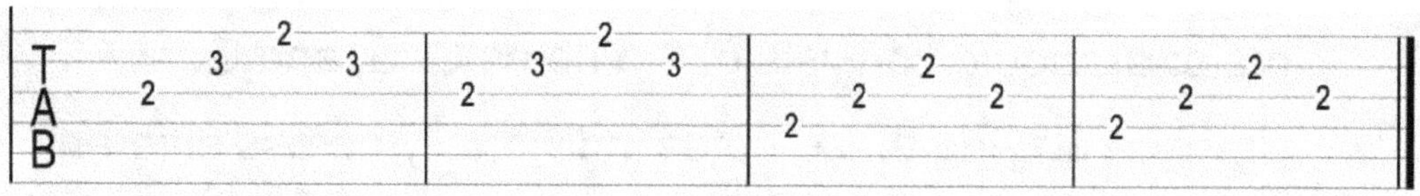

Start out with just one chord, and then progress to two chords, and so forth, when doing arpeggios. This will help you master the technique more easily and make your playing more fluid.

- **Practicing with a Metronome:** Use a metronome to ensure consistent timing and rhythm while practicing arpeggios. Start slow and gradually increase the tempo, maintaining accuracy and clarity.

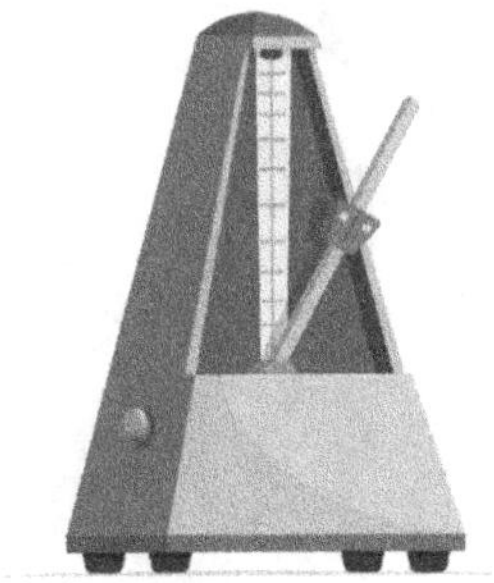

Fingerstyle Techniques

Fingerstyle guitar involves plucking the strings with your fingers to produce a rich, expressive sound. This technique is versatile and can be applied to various genres, from folk to classical. Here's how to develop your fingerstyle skills:

1. **Basic Fingerstyle Patterns**: Begin with simple fingerstyle patterns, using your thumb for the bass strings (E, A, D) and your index, middle, and ring fingers for the treble strings (G, B, E). This is the classical fingerstyle. You can also use the pick and your fingers.

- **Thumb Independence**: Focus on developing thumb independence so it can maintain a steady bass rhythm while your other fingers play melody or harmony. Practice exercises that isolate thumb movement to strengthen this skill.

- **Dynamics and Expression**: Control dynamics by varying the pressure and angle with which you pluck the strings. This adds expressiveness and dimension to your playing, allowing you to convey different emotions.
- **Combining Fingerstyle with Other Techniques**: Experiment with integrating fingerstyle with strumming. This combination can create dynamic, flowing musical phrasing and enhance the overall texture.

By mastering arpeggios and fingerstyle techniques, you'll expand your musical vocabulary and enhance your ability to convey emotion through your playing.

Chapter III Quiz

In chapter 3, you have learned about finger placement, hand positioning, basic chords, progressions, arpeggios, and fingerstyle. All are designed to enhance your picking hand.

Q: Why is finger placement so important in playing the guitar?
A: ______________________________

Q: How can a relaxed hand position benefit your playing?
A: ______________________________

Q: Why are open chords great for beginners to start with?
A: ______________________________

Q: What three-chord progression is most popular in songs?
A: ______________________________

Q: How are arpeggios beneficial to your guitar playing?
A: ______________________________

Q: What is the benefit of playing chords fingerstyle?
A: ______________________________

Chapter III summary

First, master finger placement. This is essential for forming guitar chords, scales, or intricate solos. Proper hand placement ensures you play proficiently and effectively. Preventing hand injury and better overall tone quality.

Second, focus on developing both hands and understanding the role of each. Don't just focus on the fretboard hand, as the picking hand is equally important in playing both rhythm and lead guitar.

Third, master basic chords and chord progressions. The better you develop a solid foundation, the better you will understand and play more complex musical concepts. Don't skip the basics; they provide the foundation.

Fourth, work on arpeggios and fingerstyle. These are also fundamental techniques that can develop into more complex aspects of your playing. They provide a different sound than strumming and can add a variety of emotions to your music.

Lastly, by mastering the concepts in this chapter, you will expand your musical vocabulary and enhance your ability to convey emotion across many different musical landscapes. Allowing you to express yourself more creatively.

Chapter IV: Intermediate Techniques

Lesson 10: Advanced Chord Structures

As you progress on your guitar journey, expanding your chord vocabulary is essential for expressing a wider range of musical ideas and emotions. Advanced chord structures provide richness and complexity to your playing.

Power Chords

Power chords are a staple in rock and metal music, known for their robust sound and ease of play. Unlike traditional chords, power chords are not true chords, as they lack a third. Instead, they consist of the root and the fifth.

- **Basic Power Chord Shape**: To play a power chord, place your index finger on the root note and your ring finger on the fifth note, usually two frets higher and one string down.

Work at stretching your fingers when forming these types of chords. It will benefit you in the long run.

- **Movable Shapes:** Power chords are movable, meaning you can shift the shape up and down the neck to play different chords. This makes them incredibly versatile and useful for quick chord changes.

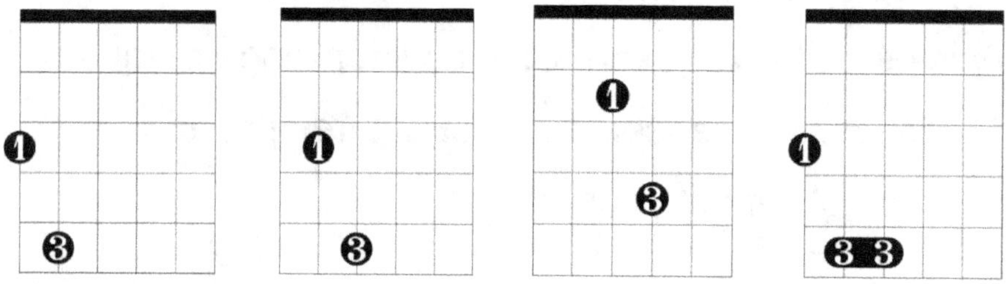

As you can see, these are all two-note chords that are very similar in shape, although they are on different strings. The last one shows that you can also play them with three fingers to enhance the chord.

- **Using Power Chords in Progressions**: Start off by playing power chords along the 6th and 5th strings. This will allow you to get used to their simplicity and how they sound as you move them along the fretboard.

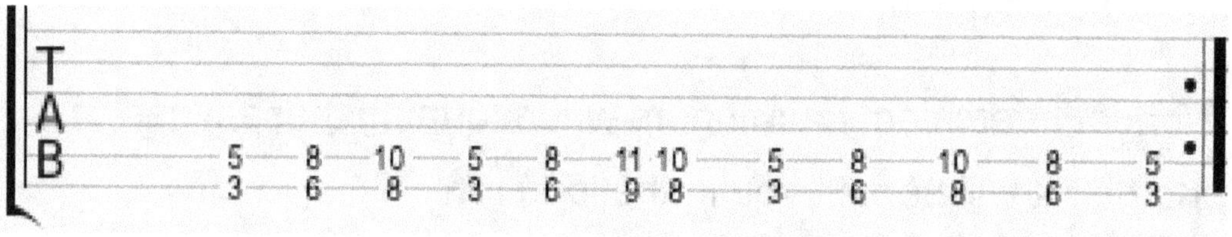

Suspended and Extended Chords

Suspended and extended chords add color and tension to your playing, making them a valuable tool for creating dynamic and interesting music.

- **Suspended Chords (Sus Chords)**: **Sus2**: This chord replaces the 3rd with a 2nd. For example, a Dsus2 chord involves playing D, E, and A.

D Major: D F# A = 1 3 5

D minor: D F A = 1 flat 3 5

Dsus2: D E A = 1 2 5

- **Sus4**: This chord replaces the third with a fourth. For example, a Dsus4 chord involves playing D, G, and A.

D Major: D F# A = 1 3 5

D minor: D F A = 1 flat 3 5

Dsus2: D E A = 1 2 5

Dsus4: D G A = 1 4 5

- **Extended Chords:** These are where you add other notes to the basic three-note triad. Creating extended chords such as 6ths, 7ths, and add9 chords.

6th chord: This chord includes the sixth note in addition to the triad. For example, C6 includes C, E, G, and A

C Major Scale: C D E F G A B = 1 2 3 4 5 6 7

C major chord: C E G = 1 3 5

C major 6th: C E G A = 1 3 5 6

7th chord: This chord includes the seventh note in addition to the triad. CM7 includes C, E, G, and B. This note also creates a dominant chord by adding the flat 7th note to the major triad.

C Major: C E G = 1 3 5

C Major 7: C E G B = 1 3 5 7

C dominant 7 (C7): C E G B flat = 1 3 5 flat 7

Master these advanced chord structures, and you will expand your harmonic palette and enhance your ability to craft compelling compositions.

Lesson 11: Lead Guitar Fundamentals

In this lesson, we will explore the essential skills and techniques that underpin lead guitar playing. As a lead guitarist, your role often involves playing melodic lines, solos, and embellishments that add depth and excitement to a song.

Playing Melodic Lines

Melodic lines are the backbone of lead guitar playing. They can convey emotion, tell a story, and complement a song's rhythm and harmony. Here are some key aspects to consider when playing melodic lines:

- **Understanding Melody**: A melody is a sequence of notes that is both memorable and expressive. Listen to your favorite songs and identify the melodies that stand out. Analyze how they use rhythm, note choice, and phrasing to create impact.

These are musical phrases that are played with single notes. They add contrast to the multiple-note chords used to play harmony.

- **Scale Familiarity:** Knowing your scales is crucial for crafting melodic lines. Start with the major and minor pentatonic scales, as they are widely used in rock, blues, and pop music. These scales provide a framework for improvisation and melody creation.

Major Pentatonic   Minor Pentatonic

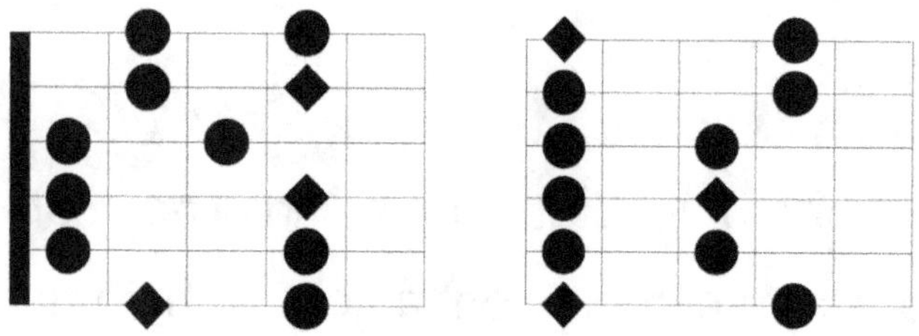

- **Phrasing**: Effective phrasing involves the timing and articulation of notes. Experiment with different phrasing techniques, such as slides, bends, hammer-ons, and pull-offs, to add expression to your playing.

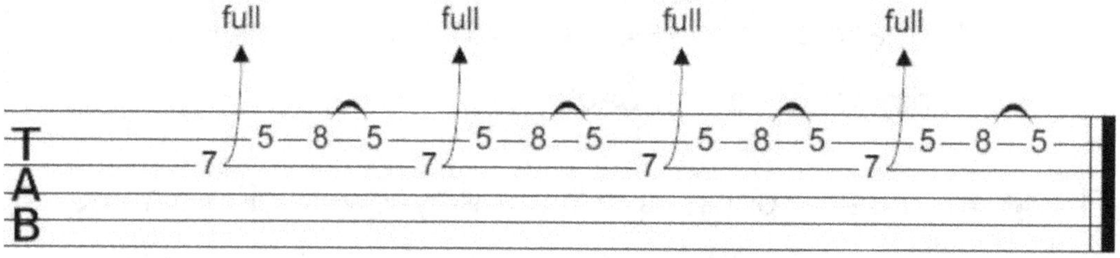

Basic Soloing Techniques

Soloing is an integral part of lead guitar playing. It allows you to showcase your individuality and technical skill. Here are some basic techniques to get you started on crafting engaging solos:

- **Pentatonic Soloing**: The pentatonic scale is a go-to for many guitarists due to its simplicity and versatility. Practice soloing over backing tracks using the pentatonic scale, focusing on creating melodic phrases and exploring different positions on the fretboard.

Play the major pentatonic scale over a major key progression, and use the minor pentatonic scale over a minor key progression. Listen to how they fit over the chords, you'll see very quickly why they are so popular.

- **String Bending**: Bending strings adds emotion and expressiveness to your solos. Practice bending notes to achieve precise intonation, aiming for the target pitch. Combine bends with vibrato for added depth.

Bending strings is a great way to add expression to a note, but it will take time to master. So be patient with this technique.

- **Sliding Techniques:** Incorporate slides into your solos to create smooth, flowing lines. These techniques enable faster, more fluid playing, allowing you to connect notes seamlessly.

With this technique, you can slide up the fretboard (ascending) or you can slide down the fretboard (descending) and cover multiple frets in the process.

String bends, slide up and down.

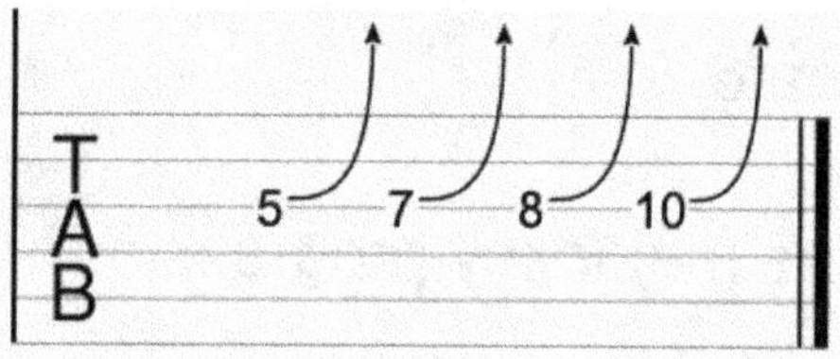

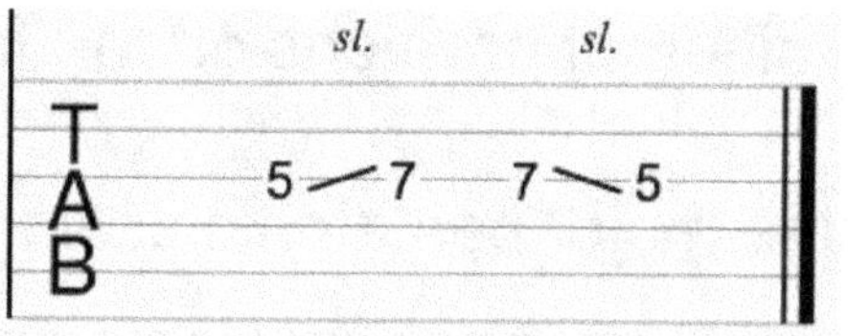

These two techniques are fundamental to lead guitar playing and essential to lead guitar phrasing, which involves combining them to craft memorable melody lines.

This slide example is on the first string. Sliding up from the 5th fret to the 6th and 7th, and then back down to the 5th. Work on this in different areas of the fretboard.

- **Hammer-ons and Pull-offs:** These are ways that you can play multiple notes with minimal effort, by picking one note but playing two due to hammering on and pulling off the other ones.

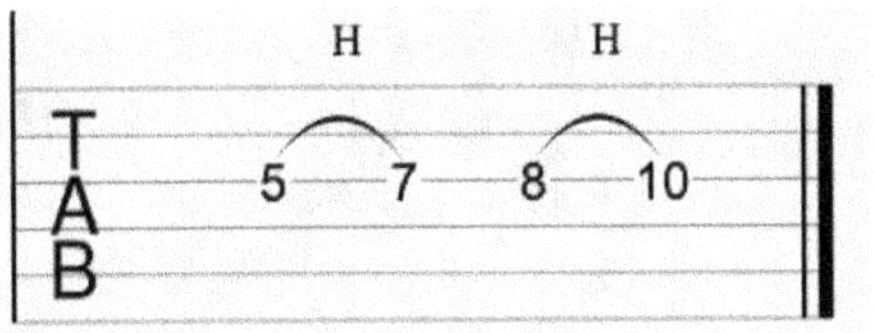

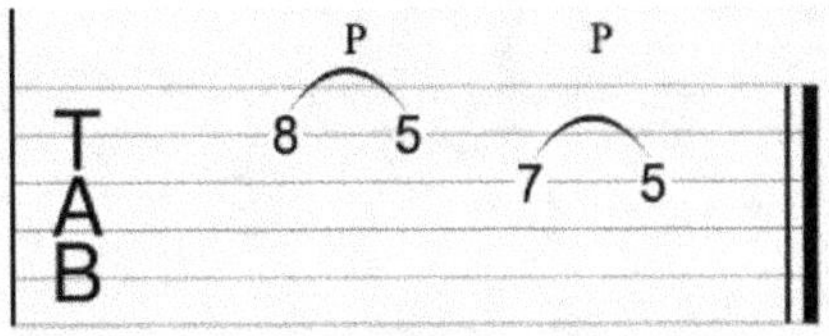

The third diagram shows how to use these two techniques together to create a hammer-on pull-off.

- **Vibrato**: A musical technique that allows you to rapidly vary the pitch of a note. Very much like a singer does with their voice. A core expressive tool used in lead guitar playing.

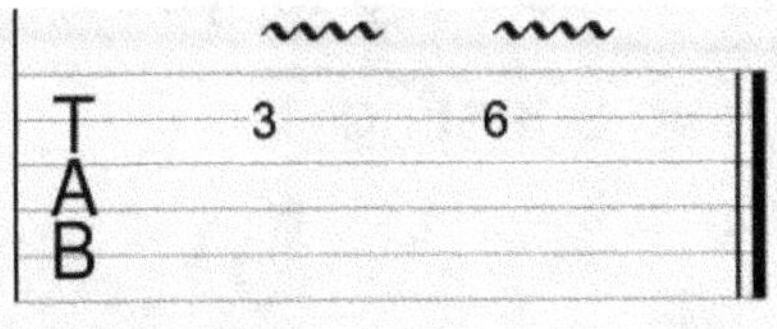

- **Combining Techniques:** Once you have mastered the techniques individually, you then combine them to craft memorable phrasing.

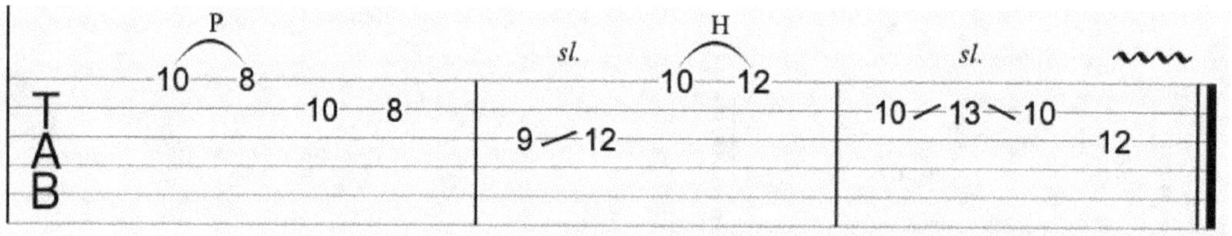

- **Improvisation**: Develop your improvisational skills by jamming with backing tracks or other musicians. Experiment with different scales, modes, and techniques to find your unique soloist voice.

By mastering these lead guitar fundamentals, you'll gain the confidence and ability to create captivating melodies and solos.

As you continue to explore and refine these techniques, you'll enhance your musical expression and leave a lasting impression on your listeners.

Lesson 12: Improvisation Skills

Improvisation is a key component of musical expression and creativity. It allows you to spontaneously create music, explore new ideas, and develop your unique guitar voice.

Scales for Improvisation

Scales are fundamental tools for improvisation, providing a framework for creating melodies and solos. Here are some essential scales to incorporate into your improvisational practice:

- **Pentatonic Scale**: This five-note scale was discussed earlier and is worth revisiting, as it is a great starting point for its simplicity and versatility. Start with the minor in different positions on the fretboard to gain flexibility and fluency.

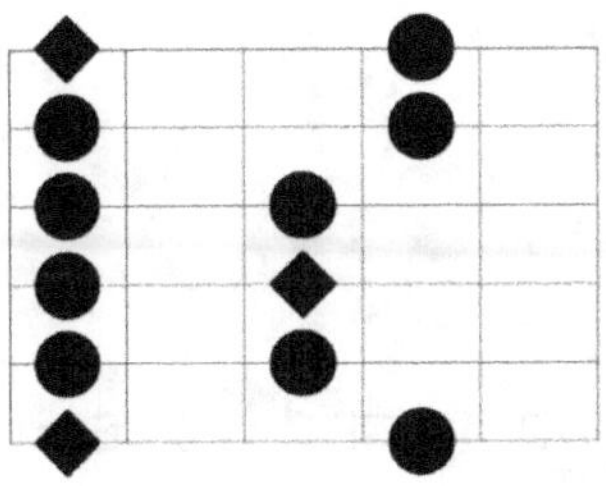

- **Blues Scale:** An extension of the pentatonic scale, the blues scale adds a "blue note," providing a characteristic bluesy feel. This scale is ideal for adding emotion and depth to your improvisations in blues and rock genres.

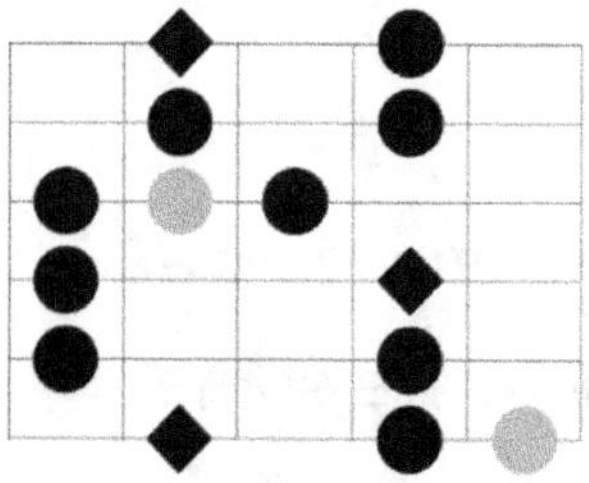
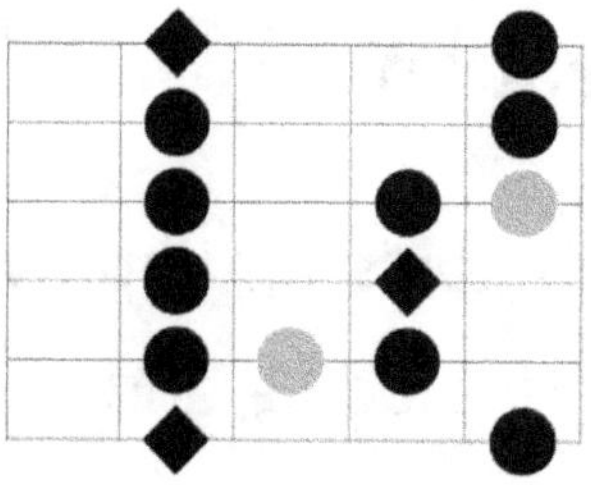

- **Major and Minor Scales**: The seven-note major and minor scales are essential for understanding Western music theory. They serve as the foundation for more complex scales and modes. Use these scales to explore different emotional tones in your improvisations.

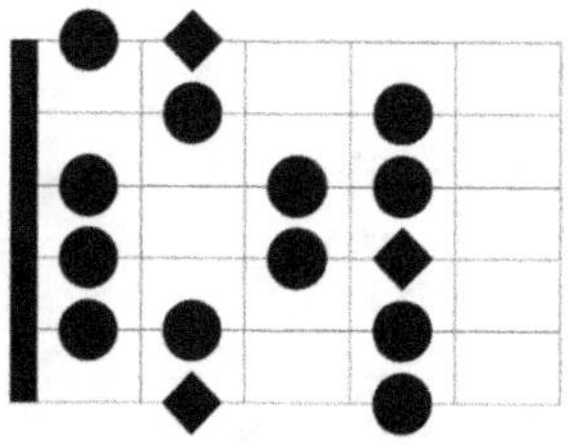
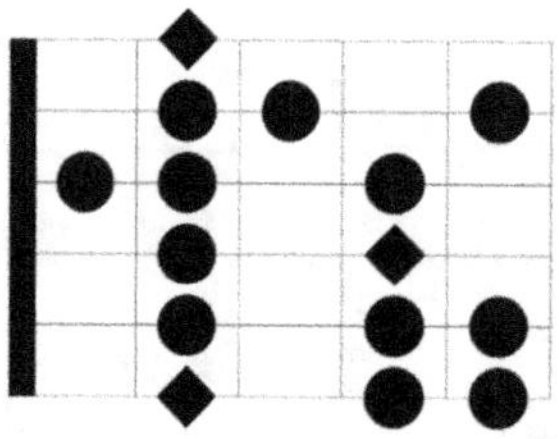

Notice how these are different from the pentatonic and blues.

- **Modes:** Variations of the major scale, each with its own distinct sound. Common modes include Dorian, Phrygian, and Mixolydian. Experimenting with modes can add variety and richness to your improvisational palette.

Dorian mode

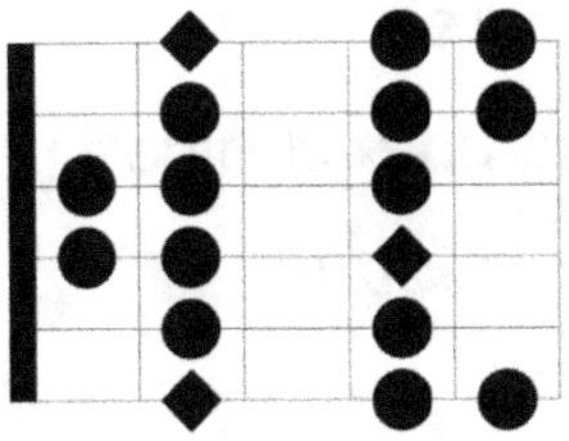

Phrygian mode

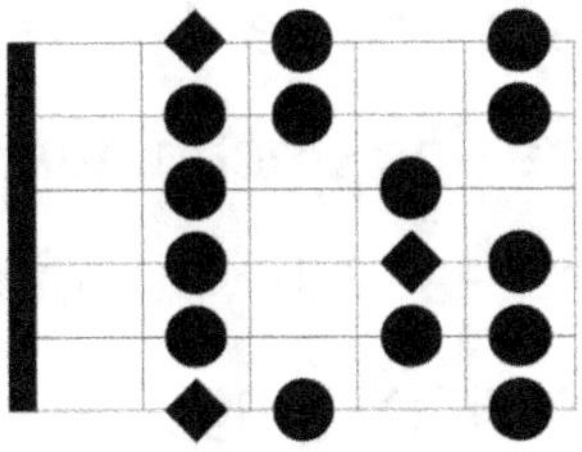

Mixolydian mode

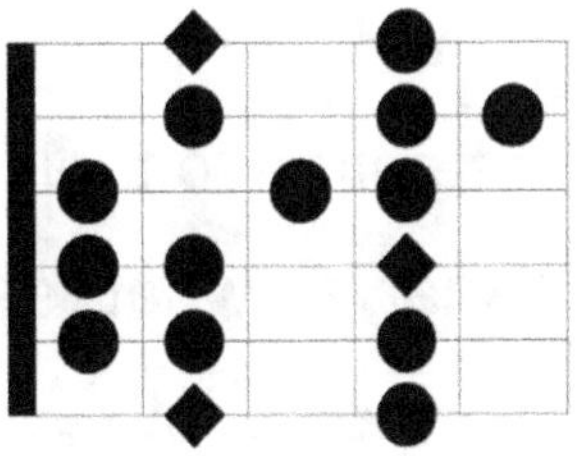

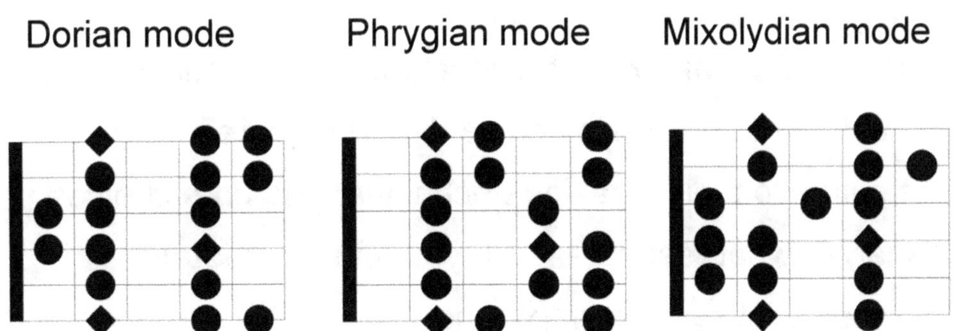

The modes are derived from the major scale. Since there are seven notes, there are seven modes. Start with the three above and eventually work on learning the rest.

The seven modes are: The Ionian, Dorian, Phrygian, Lydian, Mixolydian, Aeolian, and Locrian. These appear across all major scales and are useful for crafting a variety of guitar riffs, solos, and melodies.

Developing Your Own Style

Creating a distinctive improvisational style involves blending technical skills with personal expression. Here are some strategies to help you develop your unique voice as a guitarist:

- **Listen and Analyze**: Study the improvisational styles of your favorite guitarists across different genres. Pay attention to their phrasing, technique, and note choices. Analyze what resonates with you and incorporate elements into your own playing.

This is a very useful technique not to overlook. This application provides insight into how guitarists approach the instrument and how you can do the same.

- **Experiment with Techniques**: Explore various guitar techniques, such as bending, sliding, tapping, and harmonics. Combining these techniques across different scales and rhythms can lead to innovative, personal improvisational ideas.

Improvising is all about making it up “on the spot” and requires a lot of practice.

- **Focus on Phrasing:** Phrasing licks are crucial for musical expression. Experiment with different note durations, rhythmic patterns, and dynamics. Practice creating themes and developing them throughout your solos to maintain better listener interest.

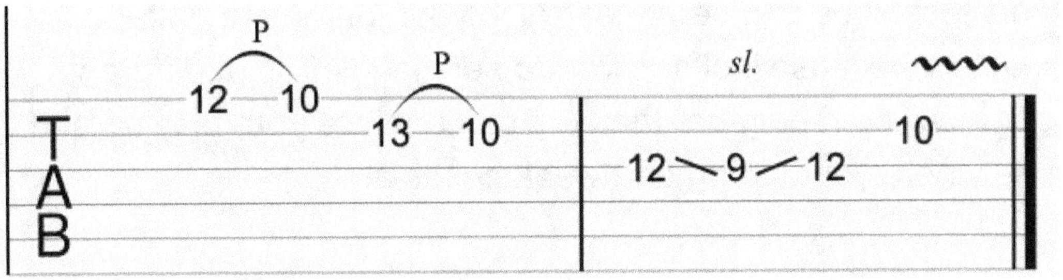

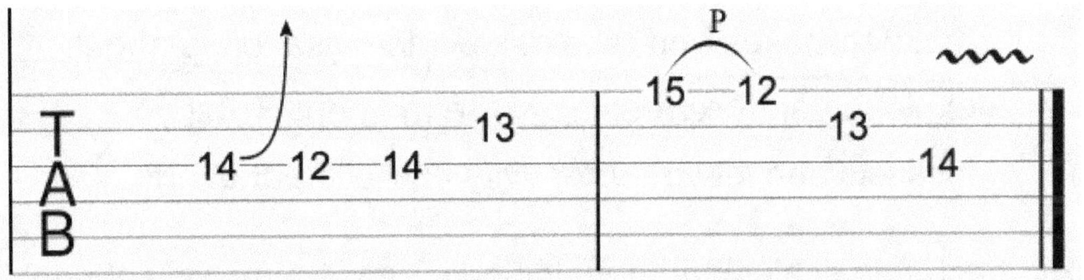

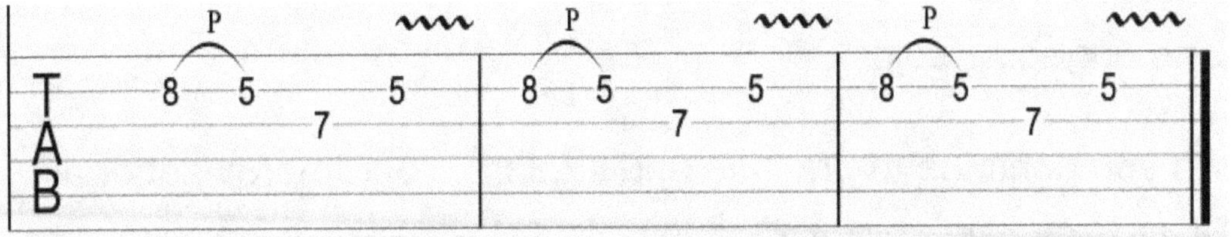

Notice how all of these use the techniques learned so far.

- **Record and Reflect:** Record your improvisations and listen back critically. Identify areas for improvement and standout moments. Use these recordings to track your progress and refine your style over time.

This technique can be beneficial in your journey to guitar mastery because it allows you to see things from a different perspective. The more that you can analyze your playing and see where your strong and weak points are.

- **Embrace Spontaneity:** Allow yourself the freedom to make mistakes and take risks. Improvisation is about exploring and expressing in the moment. Trust your instincts and let your creativity flow without overthinking.

By mastering scales and developing your own improvisational style, you'll gain the confidence and ability to create memorable and engaging solos.

As you continue to practice and explore, your improvisational skills will evolve, allowing you to express yourself more fully as a guitarist.

Chapter IV Quiz

In Chapter 4, you have learned about advanced chord structures, lead guitar fundamentals, and improvisational skills. All designed to take your guitar playing to the next level.

Q: What are power chords, and why are they so popular?
A: ____

Q: What are the two types of sus chords that alter the triad?
A: ____

Q: What is the benefit of using 6th and 7th chords for guitar?
A: ____

Q: What scales are popular for crafting solos and melodies?
A: ____

Q: What techniques are essential for phrasing guitar solos?
A: ____

Q: What does it mean to improvise when it comes to soloing?
A: ____

Chapter IV Summary

First, as you expand on your musical journey, you'll want to keep learning. This will start with expanding your chord vocabulary. Allowing you to express a wider range of musical ideas and emotions.

Second, after learning and mastering open chords, you want to move on to power chords and movable shapes. These allow you to move up and down the fretboard. Also, work on chord embellishments to add more color and emotional nuance.

Third, work on exploring lead guitar techniques. Understanding melody, developing familiarity with scales, and the techniques needed to bring them to life. Such phrasing, pentatonic soloing, and string bending.

Fourth, move into improvisational skills. A key component in musical expression and fretboard mastery. This technique helps you develop your own musical voice, which is essential for all lead guitar players.

Lastly, by mastering these concepts, you develop your own style and gain the confidence to craft rhythms, solos, and memorable musical landscapes. As you continue to practice and explore, you'll express yourself more creatively.

Chapter V: Utilizing Effects and Pedals

Lesson 13: Understanding Guitar Effects

Effects play a crucial role in shaping the sound of an electric guitar. They can dramatically alter your tone, add depth and texture, and help create a distinctive voice as a guitarist. In this lesson, we'll explore the different types of guitar effects and how they can transform your sound.

Types of Effects

Effects can be categorized into several types, each serving a unique purpose in sound manipulation. Understanding these categories will help you select the right effects for your musical style.

- **Distortion and Overdrive**: These effects add grit and sustain to your sound, making them essential for rock and metal genres. Distortion provides a heavier, more aggressive tone, while overdrive offers a smoother, more natural-sounding crunch.

- **Modulation Effects:** These include chorus, flanger, phase shifter, and vibrato. Modulation effects can add movement and width to your sound by altering the pitch or timing of your signal. They are commonly used to create lush, swirling textures.

These effects typically take the form of pedals operated with your feet and are available in a variety of shapes, sizes, and colors.

- **Time-Based Effects**: This category includes delay and reverb. Delay repeats your signal at set intervals, creating an echo effect, while reverb simulates the sound of playing in different spaces, from small rooms to vast halls.

Many popular songs use these effects. Once you know the sound, you'll begin to hear it in some of your favorite songs.

- **Dynamic Effects:** These include compressors and noise gates. A compressor evens out your playing dynamics, enhancing sustain and clarity, while a noise gate reduces unwanted noise when you're not playing.

These effects can be very useful for recording or for playing very high-gain styles of music, such as heavy metal.

- **Pitch Effects**: These include octave and pitch shifter pedals. They change the pitch of your signal, allowing you to create harmonies or simulate a bass guitar.

These effects can be very useful for broadening the sound. Create a simulation of more than one guitar. Very useful in a smaller musical ensemble, such as a power trio.

When using guitar effects, it is best to research online and try them at your local music store.

Effects can be a great way to explore new landscapes and spark your musical creativity.

How Effects Alter Sound

Each effect processes your guitar's signal in a specific way, altering the sound in distinct manners. Understanding how these effects work will help you use them more effectively.

- **Signal Path and Processing**: Effects can be arranged in various orders, creating different sounds and interactions. The position of an effect in the signal chain can significantly impact its tonal characteristics.

Once again, it is best to experiment when using pedals. That way, you can discover what pearls work best with each other.

- **Parameter Control**: Most effects include controls to adjust parameters such as intensity, speed, and depth. Experimenting with these settings allows you to tailor the effect to your preferences and explore new sonic possibilities.

By understanding the different types of effects and how they alter your sound, you can make informed choices about which effects to incorporate into your playing. With practice, you'll learn to use effects creatively, adding depth and personality to your music.

Lesson 14: Pedalboard Setup

Setting up a pedalboard is an essential step for any guitarist looking to incorporate effects into their playing. A well-organized pedalboard not only makes it easier to manage your effects but also ensures a clean and reliable signal path.

Arranging Your Pedals

The arrangement of your pedals on a pedalboard can significantly impact your sound and ease of use. Here are some tips for effectively organizing your pedals:

- **Essential Pedals First**: Place the pedals most critical to your sound and playing style at the front of your board. This typically includes a tuner and dynamic effects like compressors.

The most important pedal in the chain is your tuner pedal if you have one. Being in tune is crucial and should be prioritized.

- **Grouping by Function:** Organize pedals by their type or function. For example, place all modulation effects, such as chorus and flanger, together, and group time-based effects, such as delay and reverb.

- **Power Supply and Cables**: Ensure your pedalboard is equipped with a reliable power supply that supports all your pedals. Use high-quality patch cables to maintain a clean signal and minimize noise.

Choose a pedalboard that meets your current needs while leaving room for future expansion. A compact board is ideal for simplicity, while a larger board offers more flexibility.

Signal Chain Concepts

Understanding how to arrange your pedals in the signal chain is crucial for achieving your desired sound. Here are some basic concepts to guide you:

- **Order of Effects:** The order in which you place your pedals in the signal chain affects the overall sound. A common sequence is:
- **Tuner:** First in the chain for accurate tuning without interference from other effects.
- **Dynamic Effects:** Such as compressors, which should be placed early to shape the dynamics before any other processing.
- **Overdrive/Distortion:** Placed before modulation effects to maintain the integrity of the drive sound.
- **Modulation:** Such as chorus and flanger, which can be placed after overdrive to add movement without affecting the distortion.
- **Time-Based Effects:** Delay and reverb are typically placed at the end to avoid muddying the sound.

- **Experimentation:** While there are common conventions, experimenting with pedal order can yield unique and inspiring sounds. Try different arrangements to see how they affect your tone.

All the great guitar players' tones came through hours of experimentation. Follow suit, and you'll have great tone too.

- **Effects Loop**: If your amplifier has an effects loop, consider placing time-based effects in it to preserve preamp distortion. This can result in a clearer and more defined sound.

By understanding how to arrange and connect your pedals effectively, you can create a versatile and reliable pedalboard setup.

This will enhance your ability to shape your sound and ensure you're ready for any musical situation. As you gain experience, you'll refine your setup to suit your evolving style and preferences.

Lesson 15: Experimenting with Sound

Experimenting with sound is an exciting part of being a guitarist. It allows you to break free from traditional boundaries, fostering creativity and enabling you to discover your unique musical voice.

Creating Unique Tones

Crafting a distinctive sound involves combining elements to create a tone that reflects your musical identity. Here are some strategies to help you create unique tones:

- **Exploring Effects Combinations:** Experiment with different combinations of effects pedals. Try layering unusual pairings, such as a phaser with reverb or a fuzz pedal with delay. Each combination offers new textures and sonic possibilities.

Remember, when it comes to pedals, it's all about the process. Experimenting. This is the fun, artistic part of creating your own sound.

- **Customizing Your Gear:** Adjust your guitar's tone and volume knobs to shape your sound. Experiment with pickup configurations and consider different string types or gauges to alter your tone. Upgrading components, such as pickups and potentiometers, can also make a noticeable difference.

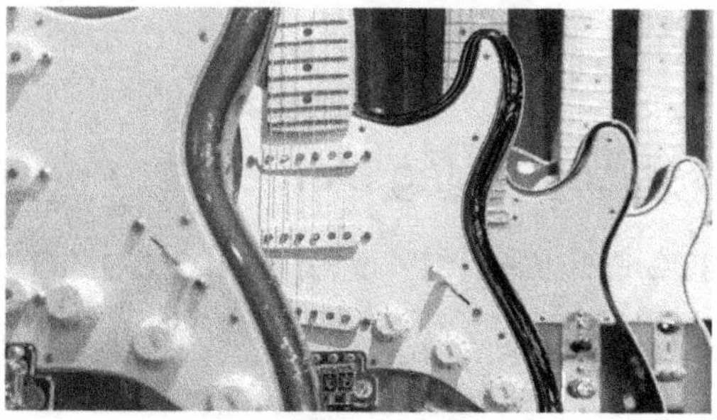

- **Amplifier Settings**: Explore the tonal potential of your amplifier by adjusting the EQ. Experiment with different preamp and power amp settings to find the sweet spot for your sound.

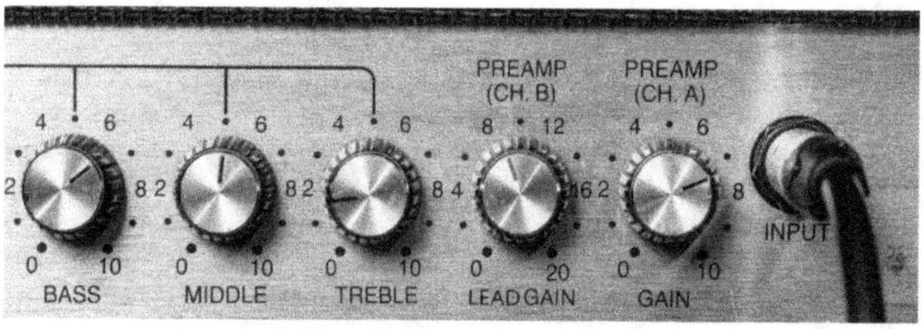

Amp settings can make a huge difference in your tone.

Alternative Techniques

These involve using your guitar and effects to create immersive, atmospheric sounds that evoke emotion and set the mood. Here are some examples to explore:

- **Ambient Effects:** Use reverb and delay pedals to create spacious, ethereal sounds. Experiment with long delay times and high reverb levels to produce a wash of sound that fills the sonic space.

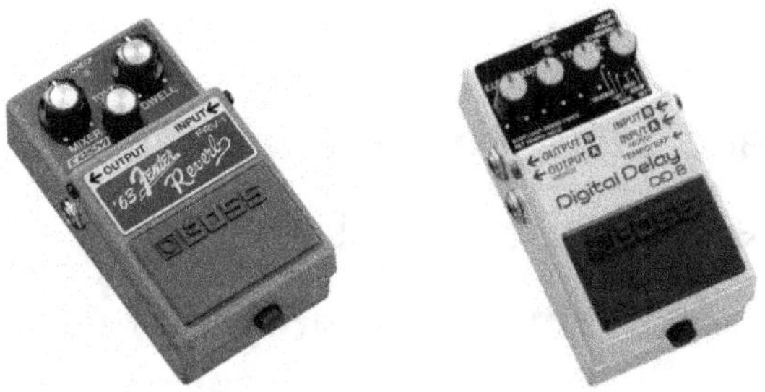

- **Looping**: Incorporate a loop pedal into your setup to layer multiple guitar parts. This technique allows you to build complex textures and harmonies, creating a rich soundscape. Use loops to craft evolving sound pieces or as a foundation for improvisation.

They also work well for looping a rhythm to play a solo over.

- **Feedback and Sustain**: Control feedback and sustain to add tension and drama to your soundscapes. Experiment with positioning your guitar relative to your amp to achieve controlled feedback, and use sustain pedals or devices to extend notes and chords.

By experimenting with sound and exploring these techniques, you'll unlock a world of creative possibilities. Listen to your favorite players and observe what they use and how they use it in their compositions.

Whether you're crafting intricate soundscapes or developing unique tones, embracing experimentation will enrich your musical journey and help you stand out as a master guitarist.

Chapter V Quiz

In chapter five, you learned about understanding guitar effects, fretboard setup, and experimenting with sound. Guitar effects pedals can help you achieve a wide range of tones.

Q: What is the difference between overdrive and distortion?
A: ______________________________

Q: How do reverb and delay effects contribute to your tone?
A: ______________________________

Q: Why is the order you put pedals together important?
A: ______________________________

Q: What is the benefit of using a pedalboard for effects?
A: ______________________________

Q: How can experimenting with the pedal knobs affect tone?
A: ______________________________

Q: How can adjusting your amplifier knobs enhance your tone?
A: ______________________________

Chapter V Summary

First, learn that the truly fun part of playing electric guitar is the use of guitar effects. These are essential for shaping the electric guitar's sound and the sound that comes out of the amplifier's speaker.

Second, you first start with your most common. Overdrive and distortion. These effects give you the base of your tone. Depending on the style of music you play, these will be the foundation for everything else.

Third, you want to learn about effects such as reverb, chorus, flanger, and delay. These can add depth and expand your signal by altering its pitch and timing.

Fourth, you want to learn about the importance of a pedalboard. This allows you to explore the best way to set up your effects and offers a great way to organize and transport them. If you decide to play any gigs in the future.

Lastly, to get the best results, take time to experiment. By doing so, you go into uncharted territory. You get to explore ways to create your very own distinctive guitar tone, as well as gain insight into some of your favorite players' guitar tones.

Chapter VI: Exploring Different Genres

Lesson 16: Rock and Blues

Rock and blues are two of the most influential and enduring genres in music. Both have shaped countless musicians and continue to inspire guitarists of all levels.

Characteristics of Rock Guitar

Rock music is characterized by its powerful sound, driving rhythms, and expressive guitar work. Here are some key elements that define rock guitar playing:

- **Power Chords**: Power chords are fundamental to rock music. They provide a strong, full sound, perfect for creating the driving rhythms rock is known for.

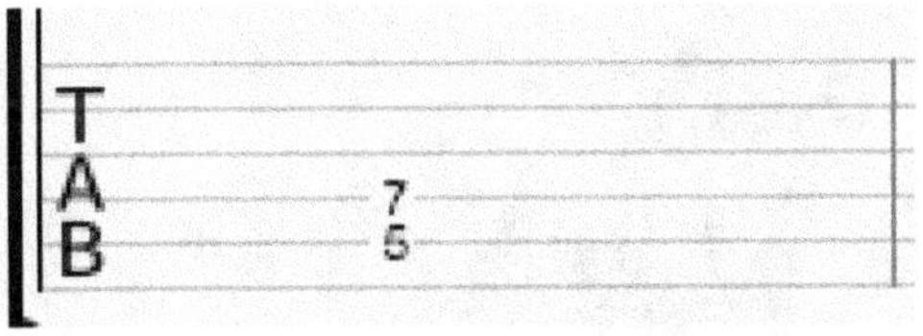

The D power chord and the G power chord. Notice how they are similar in shape.

- **Riffs and Hooks:** Rock songs often feature memorable riffs and hooks that grab the listener's attention. These are typically short, catchy melodies or chord progressions that form the song's backbone. Try creating your own riffs using scales like the pentatonic or blues scale.

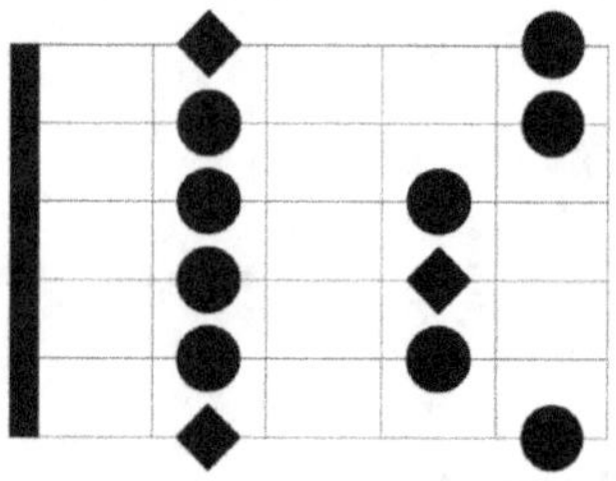

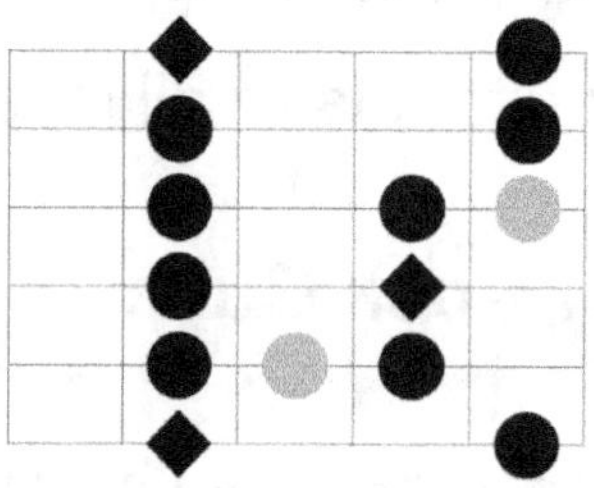

- **Distortion and Overdrive**: These effects are crucial for achieving the classic rock guitar sound. They add grit and sustain to your playing, allowing you to cut through the mix. Experiment with your amp and pedals to find the right level of distortion for your style.

Experiment with different knob combinations.

- **Solos and Improvisation:** Rock guitarists are known for their expressive and energetic solos. Focus on developing your lead guitar skills by practicing scales, bends, slides, and vibrato. Listen to famous rock solos for inspiration and try improvising over rock backing tracks.

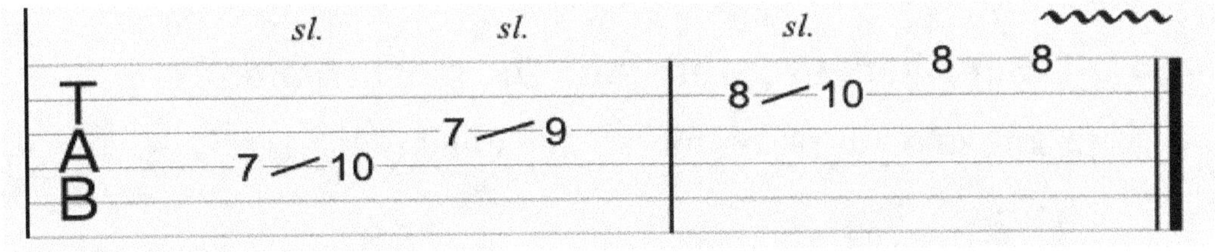

- **Rhythmic Versatility**: Rock guitarists often switch between playing rhythm and lead parts. Practice transitioning smoothly between strumming chords and playing single-note lines to enhance your versatility.

This is especially important if you're the only guitarist. You will need to learn to switch between rhythm and lead.

Blues Guitar Techniques

Blues music has a rich history and is the foundation for many modern genres, including rock. Its emotive playing style and unique techniques make it a favorite among guitarists. Here are some essential blues guitar techniques:

- **12-Bar Blues Progression:** The most common chord progression in blues music, typically using the I, IV, and V chords.

Familiarize yourself with this progression in various keys and practice playing it with different rhythms and tempos.

- **Blues Scale**: A six-note scale that adds a "blue note" to the major and minor pentatonic scales. It's a staple for blues solos and improvisation. Practice these scales across the fretboard to gain fluency and flexibility.

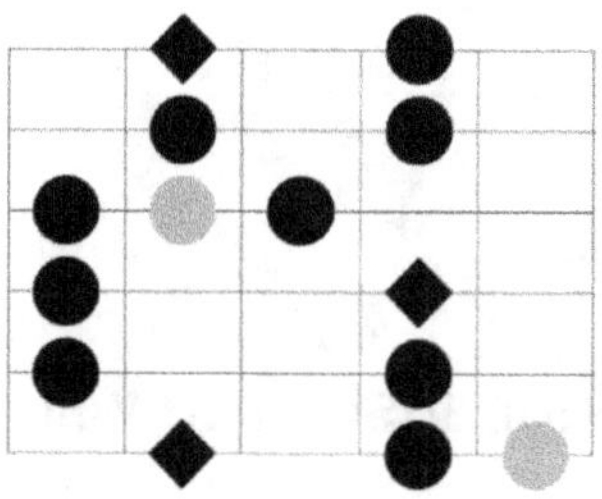

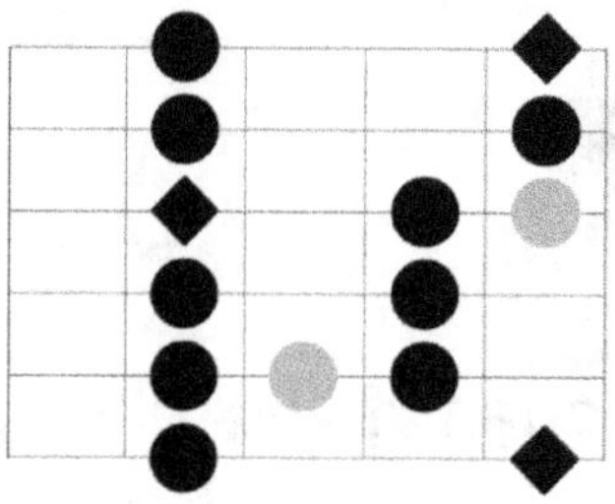

Enjoy exploring these techniques in this style.

Lesson 17: Jazz and Funk

Jazz and funk are dynamic genres that require a unique approach to guitar playing. Both styles emphasize rhythm, harmony, and improvisation, challenging guitarists to develop a refined sense of timing and creativity.

Jazz Chord Progressions

Jazz music is renowned for its complex harmonies and chord progressions. Understanding and mastering these progressions will enhance your confidence in playing jazz guitar.

- **Seventh Chords**: Jazz is rich in seventh chords, including major 7th, minor 7th, and dominant 7th. These chords add depth and color to your playing. Familiarize yourself with their shapes and sounds across the fretboard.

G M7: 1 3 5 7 = G B D F sharp

G m7: 1 flat 3 5 flat 7 = G B flat D F

G7: (dominant) 1 3 5 flat 7 = G B D F

- **II-V-I Progression:** A staple in jazz, the II-V-I progression is pivotal in countless standards. Practice this progression in various keys, focusing on smooth transitions and voice leading to maintain a seamless flow.

Key of G Major: G A B C D E F sharp = 1 2 3 4 5 6 7

The II will be the A, the V will be the D, and the I will be the G.

So the three-chord progression will be A, D, and G. Although you're playing in the key of G major, you start out on the 2nd note in the key, the A note.

- **Extended Voicings**: Jazz guitarists often use them to add interest and variety. Learn how to alter triads to create sophisticated harmonic textures.

Key of D Major: D E F sharp G A B C sharp

D Major Triad: 1 3 5 = D F sharp A

D Minor Triad: 1 flat 3 5 = D F A

Dsus2: 1 2 5 = D E A Dsus4: 1 4 5 = D G A

Triads are the foundation of chords. Develop a full understanding of them for a well-versed chord vocabulary.

Topic 2: Funk Rhythm Guitar

Funk music is characterized by its infectious grooves and rhythmic complexity. Mastering funk rhythm guitar will improve your timing and ability to lock in with the rhythm section.

- **Syncopated Rhythms**: Funk relies heavily on syncopation, emphasizing off-beats and unexpected beats. Practice playing syncopated rhythms to develop a tight, groove-oriented style.

Instead of the beat being a simple 1 2 3 4. You add syncopation by changing it up to something like:

1 2 and 3 4, 1 and 2 3 and 4, and 1 2 3 and 4.

Notice how adding the "and" within the beats changes the rhythm pattern. This is how syncopation is created. Listen to your favorite songs, and you'll hear how this is infused in the songs that catch your attention in an odd way.

Remember, mastering timing and rhythm is crucial to creating music. Master this, and you will be able to provide a solid musical foundation.

Lesson 18: Metal and Alternative

Exploring metal and alternative guitar techniques can broaden your musical palette and introduce you to new ways of expressing yourself. These genres are known for their distinct sounds, innovative approaches, and powerful riffs.

Metal Riffs and Techniques

Metal music is characterized by its intensity, speed, and technical precision. Mastering metal guitar techniques will enhance your ability to play with power and aggression.

- **Powerful Riffs:** Metal riffs are often based on power chords and palm-muted single-note lines. Practice playing tight, rhythmic patterns that emphasize precision and speed. Experiment with down-picking and alternate picking to achieve the desired heaviness and clarity.

- **Palm Muting:** This technique is essential in metal music for creating a percussive, chugging sound. Rest the side of your picking hand lightly on the strings near the bridge while playing. Focus on maintaining a consistent mute for a clean, aggressive tone.

This is an essential technique in this style of music, and you will need to master it to achieve the metal sound.

- **Fast Picking Techniques**: Develop speed and accuracy with tremolo and economy picking. Use a metronome to gradually increase your picking speed while maintaining clarity and precision. When it comes to speed and accuracy,

This can't be emphasized enough: use a metronome. If practiced daily and consistently, your playing will sound cleaner and your notes clearer. A key consideration when you're playing fast.

- **Drop Tunings**: Many metal guitarists use alternate tunings, such as drop D or drop C, to achieve a heavier sound. These tunings allow for easier power chord transitions and add depth to your riffs.

Alternative Guitar Approaches

Alternative music is known for its diversity and experimentation with unconventional sounds and structures. Exploring alternative guitar techniques can inspire creativity and broaden your musical expression.

- **Unconventional Chord Voicings**: Alternative guitarists often use unique chord shapes and voicings to create distinctive sounds. Experiment with open tunings and explore the fretboard to discover new chord possibilities.

This approach defines this style of music. Unconventional chords, progressions, and scales. Thinking outside the box, as they call it.

By exploring metal and alternative guitar techniques, you'll expand your musical horizons and deepen your understanding of these diverse genres.

Embrace the opportunity to experiment and push the boundaries of your playing, and let these styles inspire your creativity and musical expression.

Chapter VI Quiz

In chapter six, you have learned about different styles of music. Rock, Blues, Jazz, Funk, Metal, Alternative, and how they each approach the guitar differently.

Q: Why are power chords so essential in heavy metal music?
A: ____

Q: What two techniques add expressiveness to the blues?
A: ____

Q: What chord progression is most significant in jazz?
A: ____

Q: How do syncopated rhythms contribute to the style of funk?
A: ____

Q: What is the role of palm muting in metal guitar playing?
A: ____

Q: How can unconventional approaches be beneficial?
A: ____

Chapter VI Summary

First, you can expand your musicianship by exploring different genres. Such as rock, blues, jazz, funk, metal, and alternative. Each offers different concepts and techniques to expand your thinking and approach to playing the guitar.

Second, start with rock nd blues. The most influential and enduring. Both have distinctive aspects to their play. From power chords in rhythm to pentatonic scales in lead playing. As well as the very common twelve-bar progression.

Third, explore the elements of jazz and funk. What are the concepts and techniques that make these two styles unique? Both styles emphasize rhythm, harmony, and improvisation. This will help expand your vocabulary and versatility.

Fourth, explore metal and alternative genres. These can also introduce you to new ways of self-expression. Known for their distinct sounds, innovative approaches, and powerful riffs. Including palm muting, fast picking, and alternate tunings.

Lastly, you learn that by exploring different genres such as rock, blues, jazz, funk, metal, and alternative, you can massively expand your creativity and enhance your overall musicianship. Utilizing an expansive set of concepts and techniques.

Chapter VII: Playing in a Band

Lesson 19: Band Dynamics

Playing in a band is a rewarding experience that allows you to collaborate with other musicians and create music as a collective.

Understanding band dynamics is crucial to ensuring that the group functions harmoniously and produces cohesive music.

Role of the Guitarist

As a guitarist in a band, your role can vary by genre and the group's dynamics. That is why it is important to understand these concepts. Here are some key responsibilities and considerations:

- **Rhythm and Lead Balance:** Determine your primary role within the band—whether you're more focused on rhythm guitar, lead guitar, or a combination of both. Rhythm guitarists provide the harmonic foundation and drive the groove, while lead guitarists often take on solos and melodic embellishments.

If you're just one guitarist, you'll need to take on a bit of both roles. But if you have another guitarist or a keyboardist, you can share these responsibilities.

- **Supporting the Song**: Always prioritize the song over individual showmanship. Your playing should enhance the music, whether it's creating a solid rhythmic base, adding texture, or delivering impactful solos.

Utilizing chord voicings, useful scales, arpeggios, and an intentional listen to the vocal melody. Knowing when to play less and when to play more.

- **Adapting to the Style:** Be versatile and adaptable to the band's musical style. Whether you're playing rock, blues, jazz, or any other genre, tailor your approach to fit the group's overall sound and aesthetic.

Being educated in how guitarists approach the guitar in different genres will allow you to do this quite easily.

- **Communication with Band Members**: Maintain open lines of communication with the rest of the band. Discuss song arrangements, dynamics, and any changes.

It's not enough to be a great player; you must be able to communicate ideas and work with other musicians.

- **Listening Skills**: Develop strong listening skills to effectively interact with other musicians. Pay attention to the bass line, drum patterns, and vocal cues, and adjust your playing accordingly.

This is where playing with recordings and backing tracks comes in. They act as a band simulator and help you develop these skills. Work on developing these daily.

Lesson 20: Rehearsals and Performance

Playing in a band offers an exhilarating experience that allows musicians to collaborate and share their love for music with others. Successful rehearsals and performances are key to ensuring the band sounds cohesive and delivers an engaging show.

Effective Rehearsal Techniques

Rehearsals are essential for refining your band's sound, working out arrangements, and ensuring everyone is in sync. Here are some strategies to make the most of your rehearsal time:

- **Set Clear Objectives**: Before each rehearsal, establish specific intentions to achieve. This could include working on a new song, tightening up transitions, or perfecting a particular section.

Having an objective can make a huge difference in your progress. Be sure to do this to stay focused.

- **Create a Structured Plan:** Develop a rehearsal schedule that outlines the songs or sections you will focus on. Allocate time for warm-ups, individual song practice, and full run-throughs.

A structured plan helps you stay focused and productive. Allowing you to track consistent progress without burnout.

- **Record Rehearsals**: Use a smartphone or recording device to capture your rehearsals. Listening back can reveal areas that need improvement and help you track your progress over time.

This allows you to view your progress from a different perspective, very much like recording your individual practice sessions. You'll see and hear, from an audience point of view, what works and what doesn't.

While having a plan is important, be open to spontaneous creativity. If inspiration strikes, don't hesitate to explore new ideas or jam as a group.

Stage Presence and Performance Tips

Delivering an engaging performance requires more than just playing the right notes. Your stage presence and audience interaction are crucial to captivating listeners. Here are some tips to enhance your performance:

- **Confidence and Energy**: Approach the stage with confidence and energy. Your enthusiasm will be infectious, drawing the audience into your performance.

This is where practice will come into play. The more you practice honing your craft, the more confident you'll be when performing on stage.

- **Engage with the Audience**: Make eye contact, smile, and interact with the crowd. Acknowledge their presence and make them feel part of the experience.

The more fun you have while performing, the more fun they'll have watching you. For best results, get them involved and make your stage presence an experience.

- **Setlist Flow**: Carefully plan your setlist to keep the audience engaged. Balance high-energy songs with slower numbers to create a dynamic show that keeps listeners engaged.

You want your setlist to take the listener on a musical journey that is engaging and memorable.

- **Prepare for the Unexpected**: Be ready to handle any unexpected issues, such as technical difficulties or forgotten lyrics. Stay calm and adapt on the fly to keep the performance running smoothly.

There will always be a hiccup somewhere in the show. No show ever runs 100%, but knowing how to address the issues when they come up will allow you to perform as if nothing ever happened.

By implementing these rehearsal and performance techniques, you'll help create a well-prepared, captivating band experience. With practice and dedication, your band will deliver performances that leave a lasting impression on your audience.

Lesson 21: Recording Your Music

Recording your music is an exciting aspect of being a guitarist. It allows you to capture your creativity, share your work with others, and reflect on your musical growth. Whether you're recording at home or preparing for a studio session, understanding the basics of recording can greatly enhance your musical journey.

Home Recording Basics

Home recording has become increasingly accessible, allowing musicians to produce high-quality recordings without needing a professional studio. Here are some essential components and tips to get started:

Essential Equipment:

> **Audio Interface**: This device connects your guitar to your computer, converting analog signals into digital audio. Choose an interface with enough inputs to accommodate your recording needs.

- **Microphone:** While not necessary for direct input recording, a microphone is essential for capturing acoustic sounds or vocals. Consider a condenser microphone for versatility and quality.

A quality microphone is well worth the investment, so don't go lightly on this purchase.

- **Studio Monitors or Headphones**: Use quality monitors or headphones for accurate sound reproduction during recording and mixing. This ensures your final product translates well across different playback systems.

Aslo very essential for quality purposes. Invest in quality monitors and headphones. Whatever your budget can afford.

- **Cables and Accessories**: Invest in reliable cables and stands to ensure a clean signal path and convenient setup.

Also, be sure to maximize workspace and have a very organized workflow for the best results.

Preparing for Studio Sessions

Recording in a professional studio offers access to high-end equipment and experienced engineers. Proper preparation ensures you make the most of your studio time. Here's how to get ready:

- **Rehearse Thoroughly:** Ensure all band members know their parts and are comfortable with the material. This reduces the need for excessive takes and saves valuable studio time.

Recording is a different experience from playing live, so make sure to rehearse for this as well.

- **Plan Your Session**: Discuss your goals with the studio engineer beforehand. Determine the recording order, the desired sound, and any specific techniques you want to explore.

This approach will help you save time and money and provide a more focused recording session. By mastering home recording basics and preparing effectively for studio sessions, you can capture your musical ideas with clarity and professionalism.

Chapter VII Quiz

In this chapter, you learned about band dynamics, rehearsals, and performances, as well as what is required to record your artistic creativity so you can share it with the world.

Q: What is the primary role of a guitarist in a band?
A: ____

Q: Why is developing crucial listening skills important?
A: ____

Q: What effective rehearsal techniques can be beneficial?
A: ____

Q: What techniques can enhance your stage presence?
A: ____

Q: What components are essential for a home recording?
A: ____

Q: How can you effectively prepare for a recording session?
A: ____

Chapter VII Summary

First, you learn that playing in a band can be a rewarding experience that allows you to collaborate with other musicians and create music as a collective. Understanding band dynamics can enhance your success.

Second, as a guitarist in a band, your responsibilities can vary. From playing rhythm and lead, or one or the other. Look at supporting the song, adapting to the style, and communicating with the other members.

Third, arrive at rehearsals on time. This makes a big difference. Set clear objectives, create a structured plan, and record your rehearsals for analysis. This will keep you focused and on track.

Fourth, once you have that down, focus on performance. This requires more than just playing the right notes. Work on being engaging, connecting with your audience, and delivering a musical experience.

Lastly, work on recording your music. With today's technology, you can easily do this in your home. Ensure you have the right equipment and prepare properly for each session to make the best use of your time.

Chapter VIII: Maintaining Your Skills

Lesson 22: Developing a Practice Routine

Creating a structured practice routine is essential for any guitarist aiming to improve their skills and achieve their musical goals. A well-constructed routine ensures consistent progress, helps you make the most of your practice time, and keeps you motivated.

Setting Practice Goals

Setting clear, achievable goals is the foundation of an effective practice routine. Goals give your practice sessions direction and purpose, helping you focus on areas that need improvement. Here's how to set meaningful practice goals:

- **Identify Your Objectives:** Determine what you want to achieve with your guitar playing. This could range from mastering a specific technique to learning a new song or preparing for a performance.

Clearly defined objectives guide your practice sessions and provide motivation. Providing daily focus and helping you map your route to success.

- **Break Down Larger Goals:** Divide larger goals into smaller, manageable tasks. For example, if your goal is to learn a complex song, break it down into sections and focus on mastering one part at a time.

This approach prevents you from becoming overwhelmed and helps you progress more easily while building self-confidence.

- **Set Short- and Long-Term Goals:** Balance short-term goals (e.g., practicing scales for 15 minutes daily) with long-term goals (e.g., performing at an open-mic night in three months). This combination keeps you motivated and provides a sense of accomplishment as you achieve milestones.

- **Be Specific and Measurable:** Ensure your goals are specific and measurable. Instead of setting a vague goal like "get better at strumming," aim for "practice strumming patterns for 20 minutes daily and play along to three songs by the end of the week."

- **Adapt and Adjust**: As you progress, regularly evaluate and adjust your goals. Celebrate achievements and reassess goals that need more time or a different approach.

Flexibility in goal-setting allows you to adapt to your evolving skills and interests. Providing motivation, focus, and a clear path for progress. Allowing you to arrive at your destination much faster and with more confidence.

Time Management for Musicians

Efficient time management is crucial for balancing practice with other commitments and ensuring consistent progress. Here are some strategies to help you manage your practice time effectively:

- **Create a Practice Schedule:** Designate specific times each week for practice sessions. Consistency is key, so aim to practice at the same time each day if possible. Treat these sessions as appointments you cannot miss.

This will help you grow and evolve daily by avoiding time-wasting activities.

- **Prioritize Practice Elements:** Identify the most critical areas to focus on during your practice sessions. Prioritize techniques, songs, or exercises that align with your goals and allocate time accordingly.

This ensures you make the most of the limited time you have to study and practice. Focus and organization can make a huge difference.

- **Use a Timer**: Set one for each practice segment to ensure you spend sufficient time on each area. This helps maintain focus and prevents lingering on any one aspect, ensuring a balanced practice session.

- **Reflect and Record Your Progress**: Keep a practice journal to track your progress, noting what you worked on and any challenges encountered.

By setting clear goals and managing your practice time effectively, you'll create a routine that supports your growth as a guitarist. Consistency and dedication are key to realizing your musical potential and achieving the mastery you aspire to

Lesson 23: Continued Education and Growth

As you progress in your guitar journey, it's essential to continue learning and expanding your skills. Engaging in advanced lessons and workshops allows you to deepen your knowledge, while staying inspired and motivated keeps your passion alive.

Advanced Lessons and Workshops

Advanced lessons and workshops are excellent opportunities to enhance your guitar skills and connect with other musicians. Here's how to make the most of these educational experiences:

- **Seek Out Specialized Instruction:** Look for guitar teachers or coaches who specialize in areas you wish to improve, such as jazz improvisation, classical fingerstyle, or advanced theory. Personalized instruction can provide targeted feedback and accelerate your development.

- **Attend Workshops and Masterclasses:** Participate in workshops and masterclasses led by accomplished guitarists. These events offer insights into different playing styles, techniques, and creative approaches. Take notes and apply what you learn to your practice routine.

This can allow you to bounce ideas off other guitarists in real time and gain insights into how to play.

- **Online Courses and Tutorials**: Utilize online platforms that offer advanced guitar courses and tutorials. Websites that provide access to a wealth of instructional content that you can explore at your own pace.

These are an exceptional way to learn, as they also help you develop time-management and self-motivation skills that can benefit other areas of your life.

Staying Inspired and Motivated

Maintaining inspiration and motivation is crucial for sustaining your passion for playing guitar. Here are some strategies to keep your enthusiasm alive:

- **Explore Different Genres:** Experiment with playing different genres to discover new musical landscapes. Exploring styles like classical, flamenco, or fusion can reignite your creativity and inspire fresh ideas.

The reason is that different styles incorporate different ideas and ways of thinking.

- **Attend Live Performances:** Experience the energy and excitement of music firsthand by attending concerts and live performances. Observing skilled musicians on stage can be incredibly motivating and provide new perspectives on your own playing.

This will help keep you motivated to practice daily. It will also help you to gain insight and ideas for your own on-stage performance.

- **Collaborate with Other Musicians**: Collaboration is a powerful source of inspiration. Jam with friends, form a band, or participate in music projects to share ideas and learn from each other.

- **Reflect on Your Progress**: Take time to reflect on how far you've come in your guitar journey. Celebrate your achievements, no matter how small, and recognize the progress you've made. This reflection can boost your confidence and motivation.

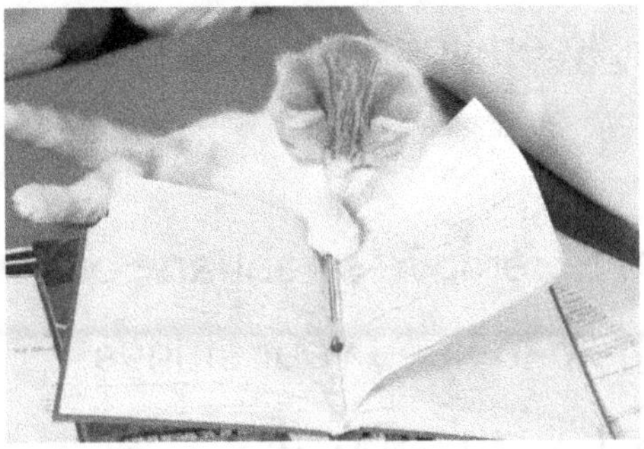

Continue looking for new ways to grow your guitar playing.

Lesson 24: Guitar Maintenance and Care

Proper maintenance and care of your electric guitar are essential to ensure it performs well, lasts for years, and continues to inspire your musical journey. This lesson will cover regular maintenance tips and troubleshooting for common issues, helping you keep your instrument in top condition.

Regular Maintenance Tips

Regular maintenance is key to preserving your guitar's playability and sound quality. Here are some tips to keep your guitar in excellent shape:

- **String Care and Replacement:** Regularly check your strings for signs of wear, such as rust or discoloration. Changing your strings every few months, or more frequently if you play often, will keep your guitar sounding bright and clear.

Wipe down your strings after playing to remove sweat and oils that can cause corrosion. This will help to keep your strings sounding and performing at their best when needed.

- **Cleaning the Body and Neck:** Use a soft, lint-free cloth to wipe down the body and neck of your guitar after each use. This prevents the buildup of dust and grime.

For deeper cleaning, use a guitar-specific polish and cleaner. Avoid household cleaners, as they can damage the finish.

- **Fretboard Maintenance**: Condition your fretboard with a suitable oil or conditioner every few months to prevent drying and cracking. Use a small amount and wipe off any excess. If your fretboard is particularly dirty, consider using a fretboard cleaner.

- **Checking the Hardware**: Regularly inspect the hardware, such as tuning pegs, bridge, and knobs, for any signs of wear or looseness.

Tighten any loose screws to prevent rattling and ensure optimal performance when playing the guitar.

Troubleshooting Common Issues

Even with regular maintenance, you may encounter common issues that affect your guitar's performance. Here's how to troubleshoot and address them:

- **Tuning Instability:** If your guitar frequently goes out of tune, check the tuning pegs and ensure they are securely tightened. Stretch new strings after installation and ensure they are properly wound around the tuning posts.

If problems persist, check the nut and bridge for any issues that could affect tuning stability.

- **String Buzz:** String buzzing can result from low action or uneven frets, as well as a change in the climate. Check the neck relief and adjust the truss rod or bridge if necessary.

If the issue persists, consider having a professional perform a setup to ensure the frets are level and the action is properly adjusted. This will ensure the guitar performs as it should when needed.

- **Electronics Issues:** If you experience crackling, buzzing, or no sound from your pickups, check the input jack and cables for connectivity issues.

Clean the pots and switches with electronic contact cleaner to remove dirt and oxidation. If you're not comfortable handling electronics, consult a professional technician.

- **Intonation Problems**: Improper intonation can cause notes to sound out of tune, even when the guitar is in tune. Adjust the saddle positions on the bridge to correct intonation.

Use a tuner to ensure each string is in tune when played open and at the 12th fret. If you're unsure how to do this, watch a video or have a professional handle it.

- **Broken or Damaged Parts**: If you notice any broken or damaged parts, such as a cracked nut or bridge saddle, replace them promptly to prevent further issues.

By following these maintenance tips and troubleshooting common issues, you'll keep your guitar in optimal condition and ensure a reliable, enjoyable playing experience.

Additional Troubleshooting for Common Guitar Issues

Beyond regular maintenance, guitarists often encounter a variety of issues that can impact their playing experience. The most common problem is fret buzz. Here is how it happens.

- **Frets Wearing Down**
- **Symptoms:** Buzzing or dead notes in specific areas of the fretboard. Over time, frequent playing can wear down frets, leading to uneven surfaces that affect playability.

If you notice these symptoms, consider having your frets leveled or replaced by a professional luthier.

- **Being Consistently Proactive**

By proactively addressing these common issues, you can ensure your guitar remains in excellent condition, providing you with a consistent and enjoyable playing experience.

Regular gular troubleshooting and maintenance will enhance your instrument's longevity and performance, allowing you to focus on making music.

Lesson 25: Achieving Your Musical Goals

Developing effective practice habits is crucial for any guitarist aiming to improve their skills and achieve their musical goals. Consistent and focused practice not only enhances your technical abilities but also deepens your understanding and enjoyment of playing the guitar.

Building Consistency in Practice

Consistency is key to making progress as a guitarist. Establishing regular practice habits ensures steady improvement and helps you stay motivated. Here are some strategies for building consistency in your practice routine:

- **Set a Regular Schedule:** Designate a specific time each day for practice. Consistency in timing helps make practice a habit. Even short, daily sessions can be more effective than infrequent, longer ones.

This allows information to stay in the mind more easily and helps the muscles form memory more consistently.

- **Create a Dedicated Practice Space:** Set up a comfortable and distraction-free area for practice. Having a designated space signals to your brain that it's time to focus on and work on your guitar skills.

- **Start with a Warm-Up**: Begin each practice session with a warm-up routine to prepare your fingers and mind. Warm-ups can include finger exercises, scales, or simple chord progressions to get you into the playing mindset.

This will keep you focused on the tasks at hand and allow you to progress more efficiently. Making the use of your time more productive.

- **Balance Routine and Variety**: While it's important to have a structured routine, don't be afraid to introduce new exercises or songs to keep your practice engaging and prevent monotony.

Techniques for Overcoming Practice Plateaus

At times, you may feel like you're not making progress despite regular practice. These plateaus are normal, and overcoming them requires patience and strategic adjustments to your routine. Here are techniques to help you break through practice plateaus:

- **Analyze and Adjust:** Reflect on your practice routine to identify areas where you may be stuck. Adjust your focus by introducing new challenges or revisiting foundational techniques that may need reinforcement.

This will help you avoid getting bored with the same tasks and becoming unmotivated to practice.

- **Incorporate Variety:** Diversify your practice by exploring different styles, techniques, or musical genres. Challenge yourself with new material that pushes your boundaries and keeps your practice fresh.

- **Seek Feedback:** Get feedback from teachers, peers, or recordings of your playing. External perspectives can provide insights into areas for improvement and motivate you to refine your technique.

- **Focus on Small Wins:** Celebrate small victories to boost your motivation. Acknowledge progress in mastering a difficult phrase or achieving smooth chord transitions.

This will keep you motivated to keep going and let you know that you are on the right track.

- **Change Your Environment:** Sometimes a change of scenery can inspire creativity and help overcome stagnation. Practice in a different room, outside, or with a new setup to refresh your perspective.

This will spark your imagination with new concepts and ideas you might not have considered otherwise.

- **Change Your Practice Focus:** Sometimes, shifting your focus to a completely different aspect of guitar playing can reinvigorate your practice routine. If you've been heavily focused on lead techniques, consider exploring rhythm.

This change can refresh your mind, introduce new challenges, and ultimately help you return to your original focus with renewed energy and insights.

- **Study Music Theory:** Understanding music theory is essential to becoming a well-rounded musician. It provides the framework for composing, improvising, and interpreting music, allowing you to communicate your musical ideas more effectively.

When you dive deeper into music theory, you will explore advanced concepts that will enrich your guitar playing and musical understanding. Familiarizing yourself with these will enhance your improvisational skills and broaden your musical vocabulary.

- **Mindful Practice:** Incorporate mindful techniques to enhance focus and concentration. Pay attention to your playing, listen intently, and be critical of technique and timing.

These are the things that will improve the quality of your guitar playing and allow you to develop mindful practice sessions.

- **Change Your Practice Focus:** Sometimes, shifting your focus to a completely different aspect of guitar playing can reinvigorate your practice routine.

If you've been heavily focused on lead techniques, try diving into rhythm guitar or vice versa. Alternatively, explore songwriting or music theory to gain a new perspective.

- **Stay Committed:** By doing so, your practice routine will employ strategies to overcome plateaus, you'll continue to progress, and find joy in your guitar journey.

Remember, every guitarist experiences ups and downs, but persistence and adaptability are key to achieving mastery. Enjoy the process and celebrate each step forward as you hone your skills and deepen your love for playing the guitar.

Chapter VIII Quiz

In this chapter, you learned about developing a practice routine, continued education, guitar maintenance, and tips for achieving your musical goals. Wrapping up this training.

Q: Why is it important and beneficial to set practice goals?
A: ______________________________

Q: How can time management enhance effective practice?
A; ______________________________

Q: Why are attending workshops beneficial to your playing?
A: ______________________________

Q: How can exploring different genres keep you motivated?
A: ______________________________

Q: Why is keeping your guitar regularly maintained important?
A; ______________________________

Q: What techniques can help overcome practice plateaus?
A: ______________________________

Chapter VIII Summary

First, you learn about the importance of creating a practice routine. This is essential for any guitarist aiming to improve their skills and achieve their musical goals. A well-constructed routine ensures efficient daily progress.

Second, you set practice objectives. Break them down into short- and long-term, and ensure they are measurable and time-bound. This will allow you to track your progress and see exactly where you are.

Third, you learn about the importance of continued education and growth. This can be done through specialized instruction, attending workshops, online courses, and guitar player communities.

Fourth, you learn more about maintaining your guitar and the benefits of doing so. This preserves the instrument's playability and sound quality. Beyond string changes and keeping it clean, you want to maintain fret buzz and tuning stability.

Lastly, you learn how to achieve your musical goals. Like building consistency in your practice, establishing a regular workspace, and making the most of your time. Start with warm up and balance your routine with variety.

Electric Guitar Mastery: Conclusion

Congratulations on reaching the end of the "Beginner's Guide to Electric Guitar Mastery"! You've taken significant steps in developing your skills and understanding of the electric guitar, and in building the confidence to do so.

Remember, mastery is a journey, not a destination. Continue practicing, exploring new techniques, and enjoying the music you create. With dedication and passion, your guitar playing will continue to grow and bring joy to you and your listeners alike.

One of the most rewarding aspects of playing the electric guitar is becoming part of the vibrant musical community. Whether you're jamming with friends, collaborating with a band, or sharing your music online. All can be very beneficial.

As you continue your guitar journey, remember that there is always more to learn and discover. The music industry is vast and diverse, offering endless opportunities for growth and creative expression.

Embracing new challenges will not only enhance your skills but also keep your playing fresh and exciting. Stay curious and open to new experiences, and allow them to shape your unique musical identity.

Take time to reflect on how far you've come since you first picked up the electric guitar. Acknowledge the progress you've made, the skills you've acquired, and the challenges you've overcome. Reflecting on your journey helps you appreciate your achievements and sets the stage for future growth.

Keep a journal of your musical experiences, noting your goals, accomplishments, and areas for improvement. This reflection will serve as a source of motivation and remind you of the joy and fulfillment that playing the guitar brings.

Seek out new resources, teachers, and experiences that challenge and inspire you. By maintaining a growth mindset and a passion for learning, you'll continue to evolve as a musician and keep the flame of creativity burning brightly.

To all your success,

Sincerely, Dwayne Jenkins

Other Books From Dwayne Jenkins

Learn Guitar Scale Theory:

Dive deep into guitar scale theory with this easy to learn from, comprehensive guidebook. An understanding of theory can add a rich vocabulary for both harmony and melody.

Learning guitar scale theory will help you expand your improvisation skills, enhance your scale vocabulary, and deepen your understanding of intervals.

Learn To Play Rhythm Guitar:

A comprehensive training course for learning chords, chord progressions, strumming, arpeggiated picking, and all things needed to be a great rhythm guitar player.

With a step-by-step system and your desire to learn, you'll be playing quickly and easily. Before you know it, you will improve your musicianship, timing, and rhythm.

Learn Guitar Chord Theory:

Have you ever looked at notation and wondered what a Cadd9 chord is? Or possibly a Gsus4? If you have one, this book explains what it is, how to create it, and how to use it.

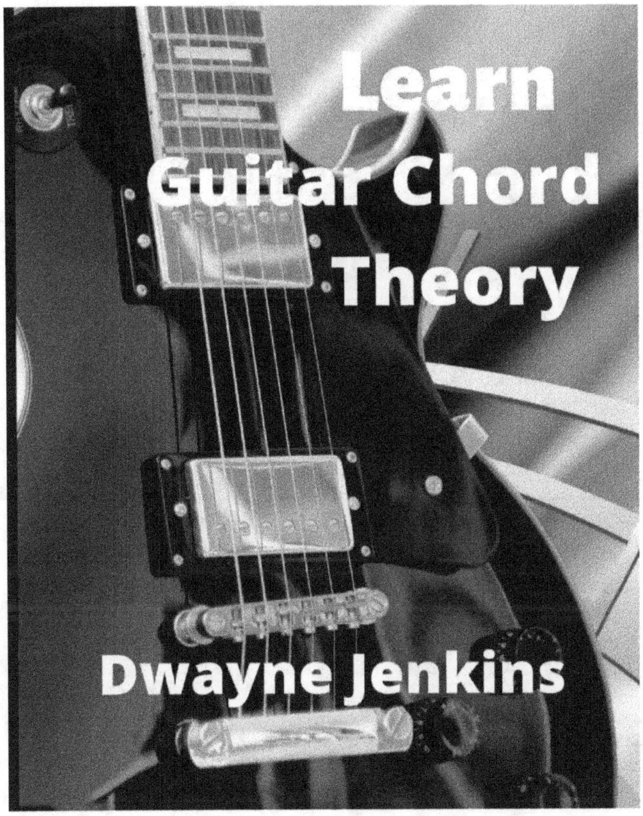

Learn Guitar Chord Theory is a comprehensive study guide on the inner workings of guitar chords. Take the time to develop your chord vocabulary and mix it with a complete understanding of how they work, and you'll become a much better player.

All books are authored by Dwayne Jenkins, published by Tritone Publishing, and are available worldwide.

Digital formats of all titles are also available for quicker learning. Just download them onto your computer and start learning right away.

Self-study is a great way to learn, as it allows you not only to go at your own pace but also to develop self-discipline and time management, which can benefit you in other areas of your life.

Also, check out Dwayne's Guitar Lessons video channel on YouTube. These are free lessons covering a wide range of guitar topics.

Whether you are working on rhythm, lead, theory, or guitar maintenance, it is all here in these lessons. These are available 24 hours a day, 7 days a week, 365 days a year.

If more help is needed, Dwayne also offers one-on-one coaching on his website.

www.DwaynesGuitarLessons.com

Best of luck, and be sure to have fun.

About the Author

Dwayne Jenkins is a guitar teacher with a unique, engaging approach that helps students of all ages and skill levels enjoy playing the guitar and ukulele. His enthusiasm and love for teaching shine through every lesson that he creates.

His lessons are designed to help you progress. No matter your reason for learning, there will always be something in Dwayne's books and products to help you achieve your dreams.

So if you're a student looking to start or a student looking to further your education, be sure to get involved with Dwayne's guitar lessons and learn what so many people have already discovered: why learning to play the guitar is one of the most incredible things you can do for yourself.

What Students Are Saying About Dwayne's Guitar Lessons

"Dwayne, thank you so much for everything you have taught me and done for me. You are an amazing guitarist and wonderful teacher". BJ

"Dwayne, it has been a true pleasure to have you at our house each week! Ken & Trevor have learned so much through you and your teachings. Thank you!" Lisa

"Dwayne, thank you for being a great teacher and teaching me many great songs. This is a skill that will last me a lifetime." Danielle

"Dwayne, we want you to know we are honored to have you at the studio. We appreciate all that you do and are grateful that we can leave you in charge." Angie & Wilson M.E.C.

"Dwayne, we are so glad you are our Teacher. It's been three years already, can you believe it? Thank you again. You're the best!" Chelsey & Lucas.

"Dwayne, we are so glad that you are in our lives. Chelsey & Lucas enjoy their time with you and look up to you. Looking forward to another great year!" Love and best wishes, Ken & Sue.

"Dwayne, thank you so much for being not only an awesome guitar teacher but an awesome friend as well," Kayla said.

"Dwayne, thank you so much for all the years of doing lessons. You have been very patient with my progress, helped me build confidence, and inspired me to pursue my dreams. And in doing so, you have become a great friend." Jake.

"Dwayne, thank you for teaching Nick guitar so well. He loves it and is getting quite good, fast. I'm amazed!" Jane.

"Dwayne, thank you so much for teaching me every Saturday, and not only teaching me guitar but also about life, and helping me with setting my goals. You are a great teacher, mentor, and the best friend ever." Carson.

"There is no other person I would want to teach me a guitar! His 1-on-1 teaching makes learning guitar very personal & exhilarating. He teaches at your pace and takes pride in what YOU want to learn. The best part is that if Dwayne doesn't know a song a student wants to play, he takes time out of the week to learn it. His teaching comes to life in my performance and has progressed over the last 8 years. Words cannot describe how amazing a teacher, rockstar, and true friend Dwayne has become to me." Dominic.

Resource Guide

The Five Major Pentatonic Scales

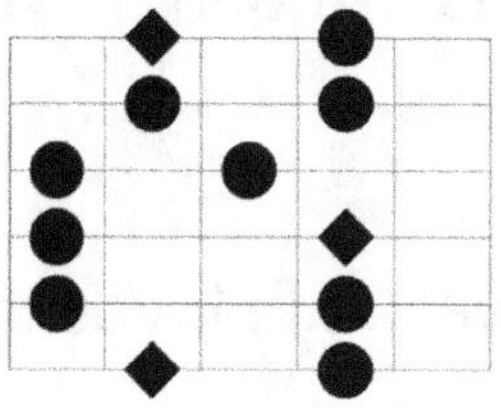

Pattern 1

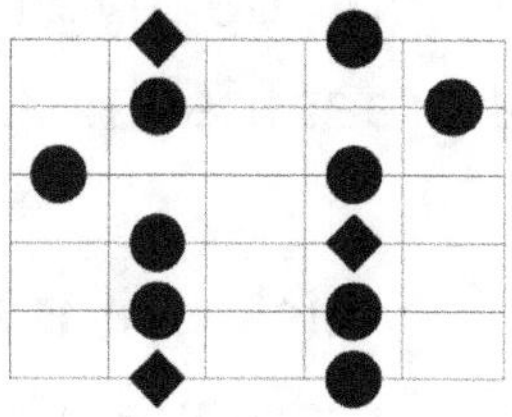

Pattern 2

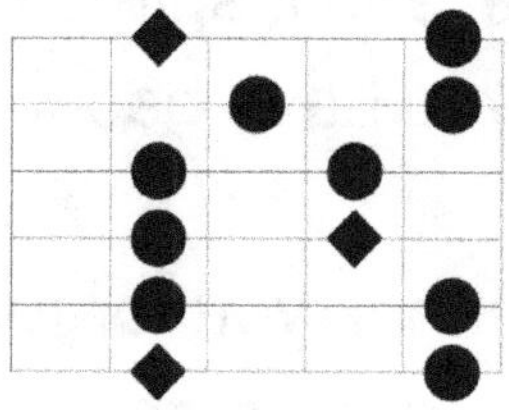

Pattern 3

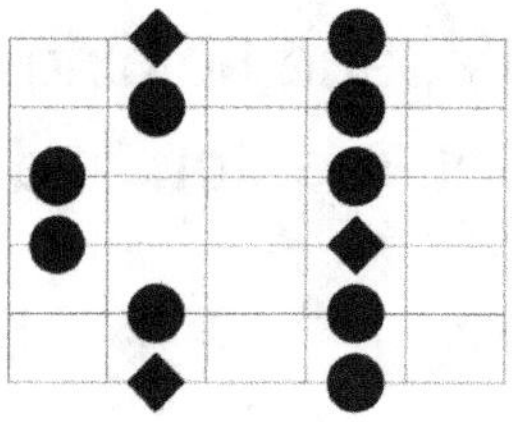

Pattern 4

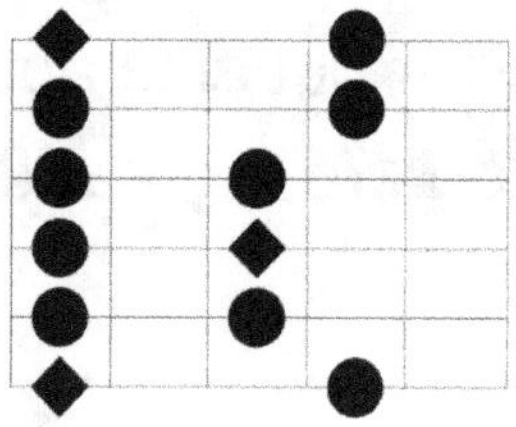

Pattern 5

Things to remember:

1. It is a five-note scale that produces a bright, happy sound.
2. The number value is 1 2 3 5 6.
3. Key Example, C Major: C D E G A
4. Created by eliminating the 4th and 7th notes of the major.
5. Each pattern starts on a tone degree of the scale.

The Five Minor Pentatonic Scales

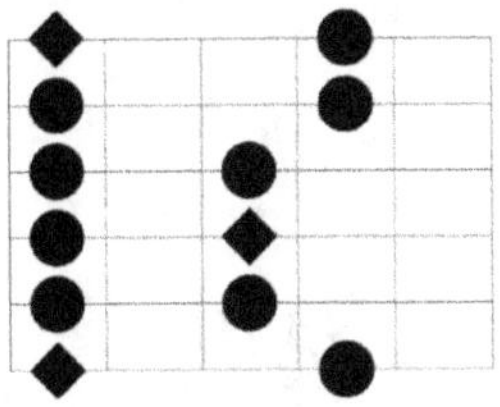

Pattern 1

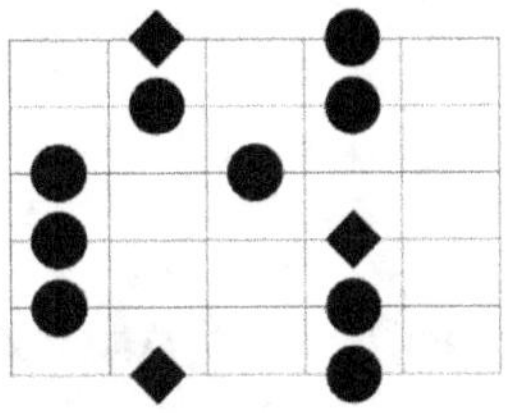

Pattern 2

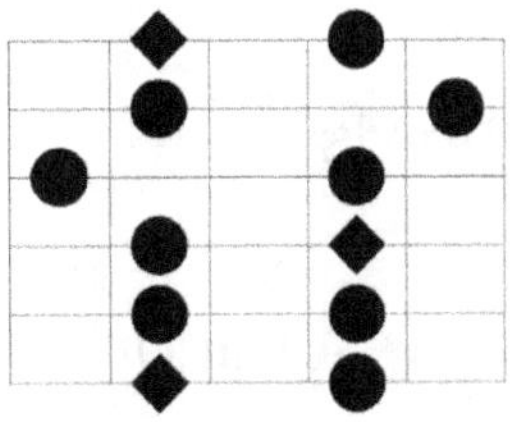

Pattern 3

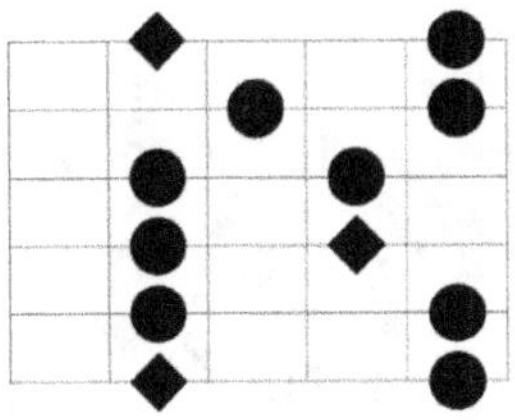

Pattern 4

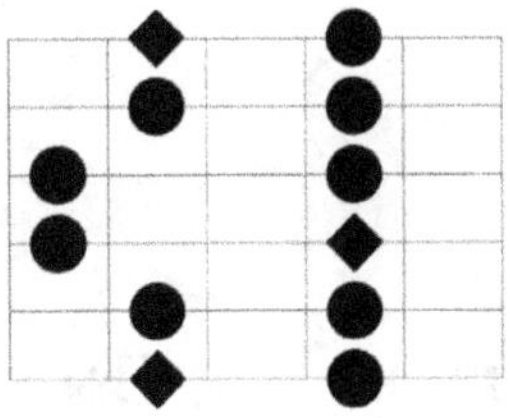

Pattern 5

1. It is a five-note scale that produces a sad, somber sound.
2. The number value is 1 flat 3 4 5 flat 7
3. Key example, A minor: A C D E G
4. Created by eliminating the 2nd and 6th of the major.
5. Each pattern starts on a tone degree of the scale.

These five-note scale patterns are essential for lead guitar mastery. Once you get these down, move on to mastering the blues scales and the modes.

Although simple, do not overlook their potency. Many great blues and rock guitarists use them.

Resource Guide

Common chords

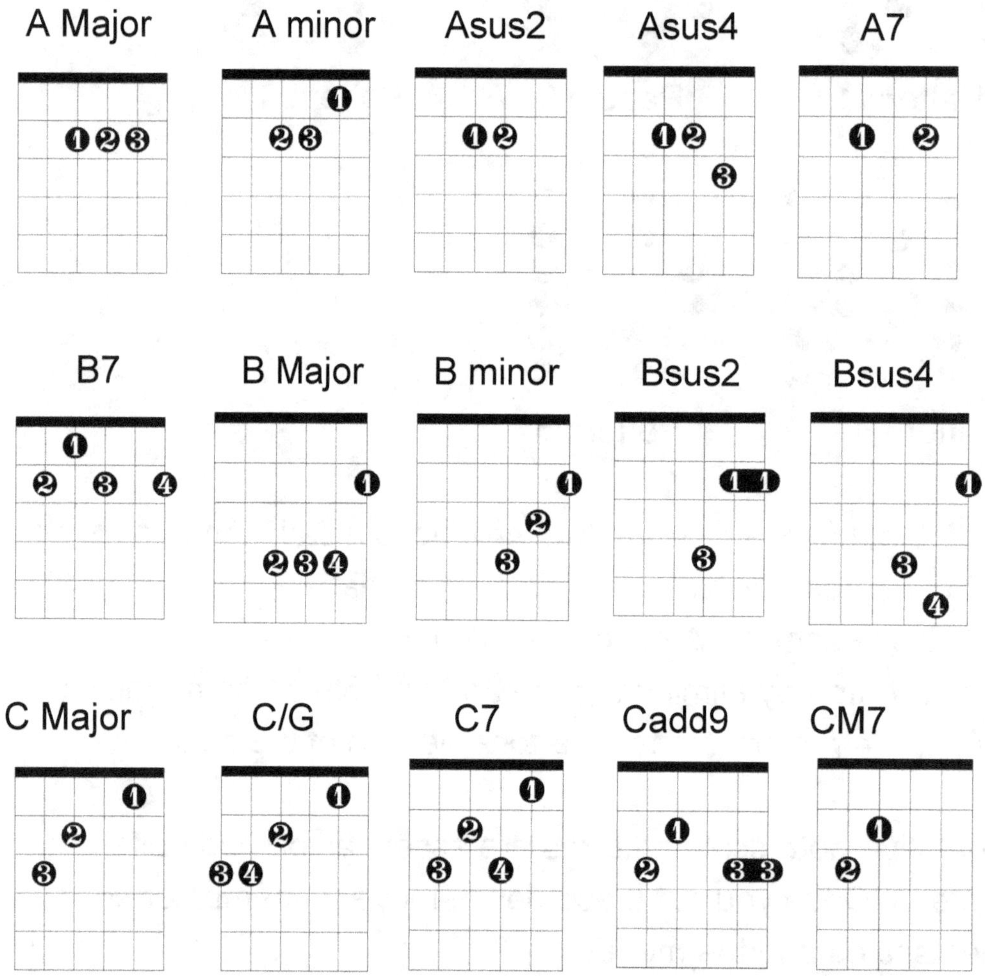

These are all chords found in many of your favorite songs. Learn them and have them handy for when needed.

Resource Guide Continued

D Major

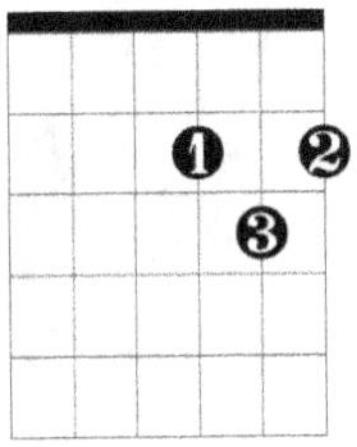

D minor

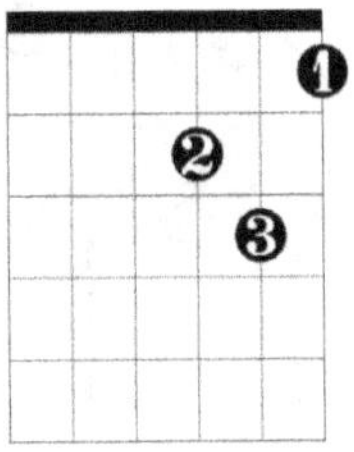

D7

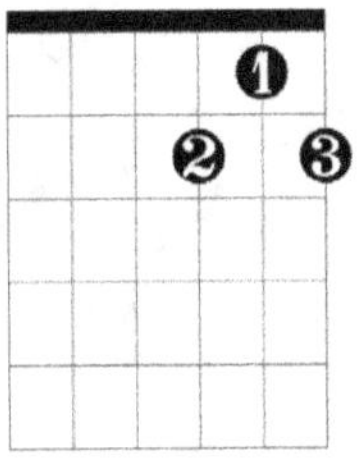

Dsus2

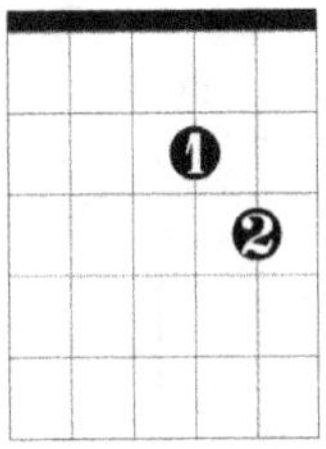

Dsus4

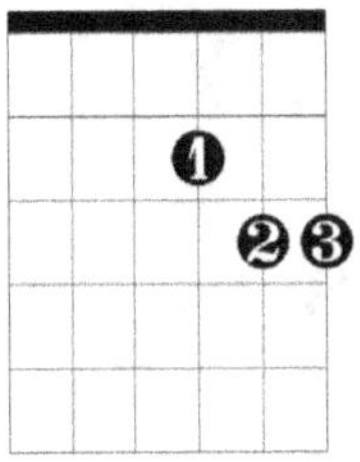

E Major

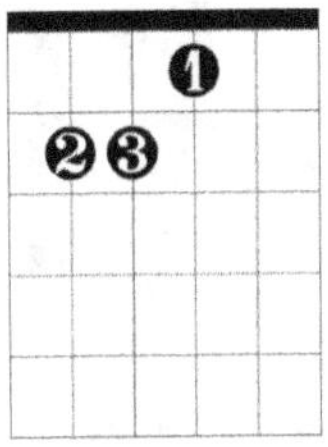

E minor

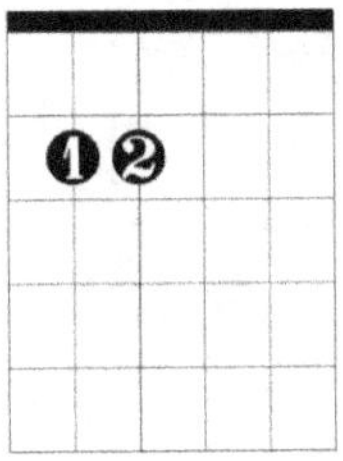

E7

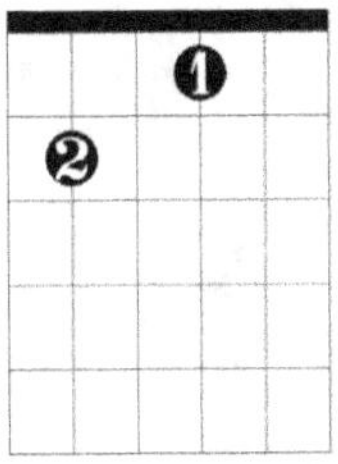

Esus4

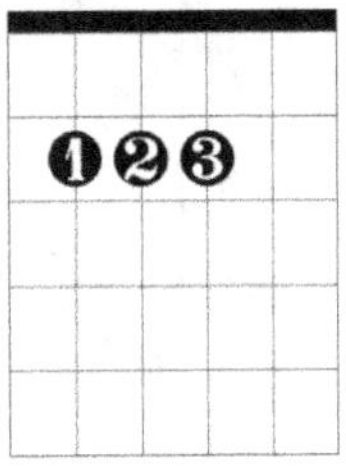

F Major

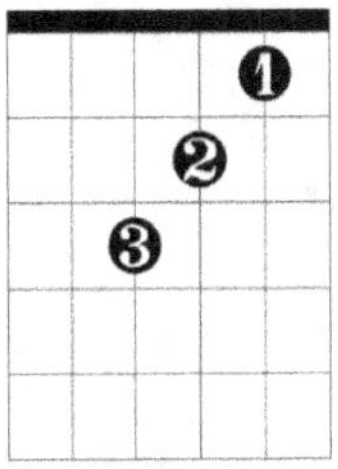

F sharp

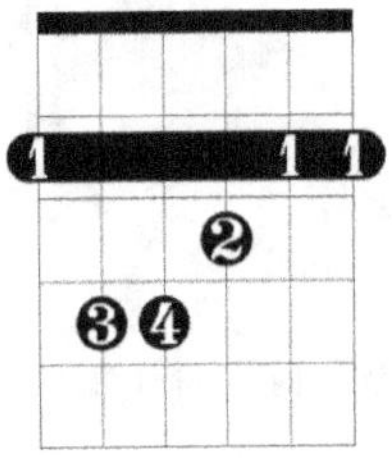

F7

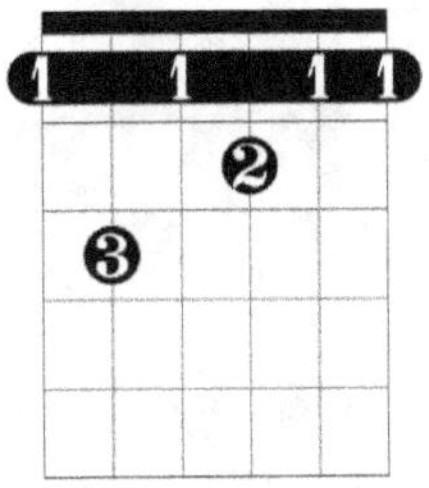

G Major

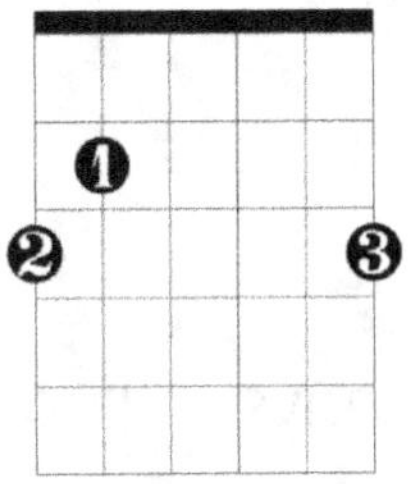

G7

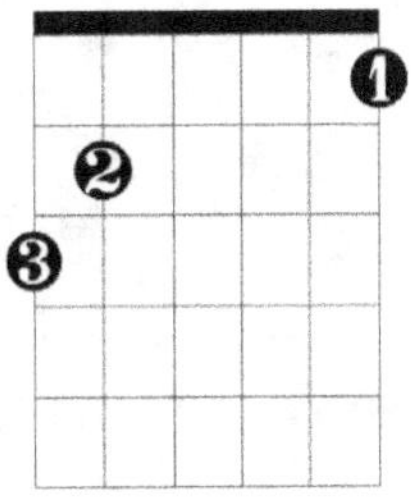

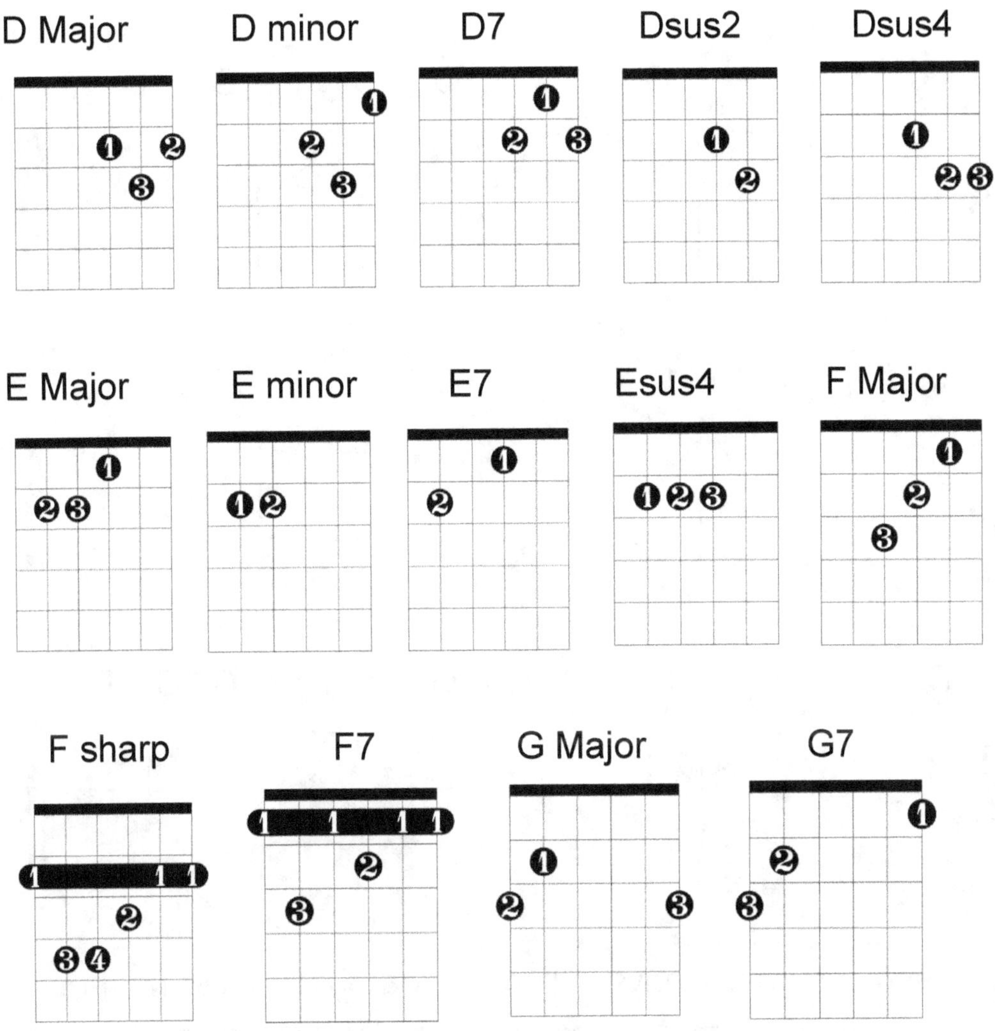

The F sharp and F7 are barre chords and are played with your index finger barring across all six strings. Not easy to start with, but very beneficial in the long run.

Resource Guide Continued

12-Bar Blues Progression: I-IV-V Key of G major = G C D

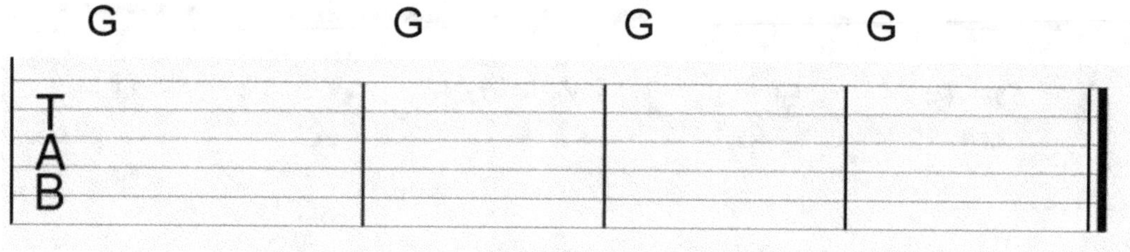

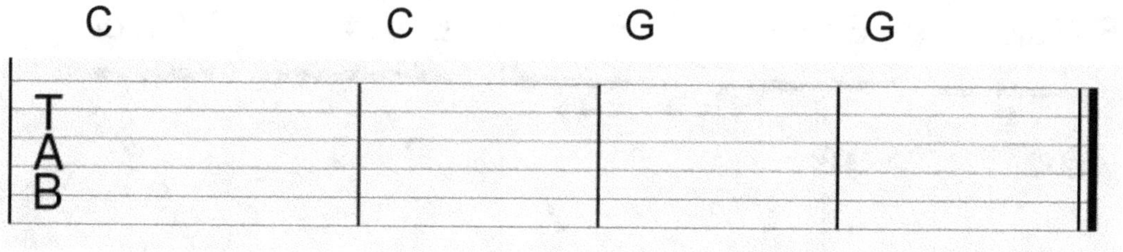

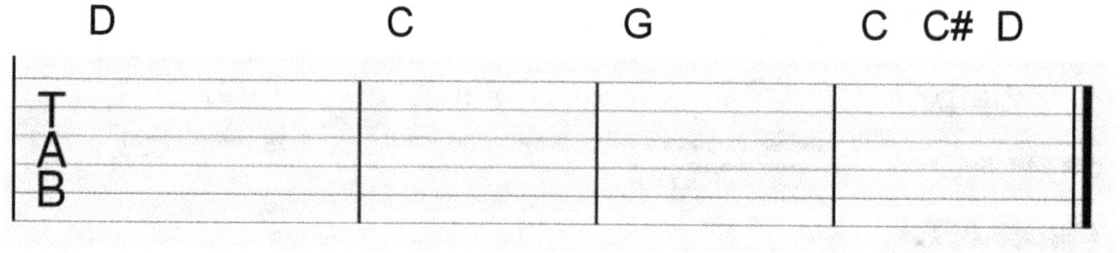

The last measure is what's called a turnaround. Utilizing the flat 5th chord. Common in the blues, and takes you back to the root chord to start all over.

Practice this progression in different keys with different chords, and always use the 1st, 4th, and 5th chords of the key.

www.ingramcontent.com/pod-product-compliance
Lightning Source LLC
Chambersburg PA
CBHW081217130726
47997CB00009B/2695
* 9 7 9 8 9 9 8 5 3 3 4 7 1 *